Please return or renew this item  by the last date shown. You may return items to any East Sussex Library. You may renew books by telephone or the internet.

0345 60 80 195 for renewals
0345 60 80 196 for enquiries

Library and Information Services
eastsussex.gov.uk/libraries

TOP 10 ATTRACTIONS

Kennedy Space Center Always worth seeing, whether or not there's a shuttle launch *(page 44)*

Walt Disney World Resort The ultimate theme park is must-see *(page 51)*

Jungle Gardens Mingle with flamingos at one of Florida's beautiful botanical gardens *(page 74)*

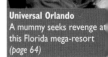

Universal Orlando A mummy seeks revenge at this Florida mega-resort *(page 64)*

ami Beach One of America's pre-eminent beach resorts, th glamor, glitz, and Art Deco aplenty *(page 25)*

St Augustine Stroll the streets and soak up the atmosphere of old Florida *(page 47)*

e Norton Museum of Art ine Impressionist and st-Impressionist works in est Palm Beach *(page 43)*

Everglades National Park Take an airboat ride and explore its unique watery world *(page 69)*

sch Gardens This theme k is home to thrilling ler coasters, African mals, and much more ge 79)*

Key West Experience its laid-back life and follow in the footsteps of Ernest Hemingway *(page 37)*

CONTENTS

72

99

24

INTRODUCTION

Mention Florida, and what comes to mind? The aptly nick-named 'Sunshine State' is best known for hundreds of miles of beautiful beaches and its man-made attractions, notably Walt Disney World near the center of the state, one of the most popular resort destinations in the world.

But if you look further, the state's vast and varied landscape offers an endless number of opportunities, from a canoe trek in North Florida to snorkeling in the warm waters of the Florida Keys. The state stretches almost 450 miles (720km) long and 130 miles (200km) wide, with a diverse terrain – long stretches of seashore, inland rivers, dense woodland, countless lakes, and primitive wetlands. The highest point is only 345ft (105m) above sea level; from any point in Florida a beach is no more than 60 miles (97km) away.

History buffs can find plenty to take pleasure in, from picturesque St Augustine, the oldest continuously settled city in North America (founded 55 years before the Pilgrims landed at Plymouth Rock in 1620), to 21st-century happenings at Kennedy Space Center. Visitors looking for city life can head to Miami, Tampa, or Jacksonville. Sports fans can water-ski, fish, swim, surf, dive, golf, surf, canoe, and hike. Many upscale resorts feature sports clinics and spa facilities.

By the Compass

Depending on where you travel in the state, Florida can be sleepy and subtropical or fast and trendy. As you plan a holiday, it is helpful to look at the state as eight separate regions, starting in **Northwest Florida**, where the Panhandle (named because of its shape) stretches from Pensacola on the western

Gulf Coast sunset

Coastal dimensions

After Alaska, Florida has the second-longest coastline of any US state – 1,197 miles (1,926km).

border of the state to the town of Apalachicola. Best known for miles and miles of undeveloped beaches with powdery-white sand, this area is acclaimed as one of the most beautiful in the United States, featuring quiet fishing towns and secluded beach communities.

North Central Florida is home to the state capital, Tallahassee, with a rich sense of history, and rolling hills, ancient oaks, lakes, and springs. Sleepy fishing villages draw vacationers who want to fish, boat, hunt, camp, and hike.

Historical St Augustine's charms and beautiful Amelia Island are the top draws in **Northeast** Florida, where the Right whales return every fall to give birth in the Atlantic Ocean.

Central Florida, from Ocala to the shores of Lake Okeechobee, is home to Walt Disney World, SeaWorld Orlando, Universal Orlando, and other family-friendly attractions. But there are plenty of off-the-beaten path adventures, too; just miles away from the man-made playgrounds is Ocala National Forest, a magnificent preserve with a host of wildlife.

Head due east to **Central East Florida**, also known as the Space Coast. Vacationers still surf in the warm Atlantic and drive their cars on world-famous Daytona Beach, but further south Kennedy Space Center is the big draw, where visitors get a close view of the space shuttle and can climb aboard a replica. Canaveral National Seashore's pristine beaches are just a few minutes' drive from the launch pad.

Central West Florida curves along the Gulf of Mexico, with family-friendly beaches and many of the state's top cultural sights in Tampa, St Petersburg, and Sarasota.

Due south of Sarasota, **Southwest Florida** has some of the prettiest beaches on the calm Gulf of Mexico, and seashells by the handful on Sanibel and Captiva islands. Some of the

Sea shells on the seashore

state's best fishing is here, as well as the Everglades National Park – more than 1.4 million acres (560,000 hectares) between Miami and Naples – home to more than 400 species of birds, 25 species of mammals, and 125 species of fish.

Back across to the Atlantic coast, **Southeast Florida** includes chic Palm Beach, where millionaires still congregate in the winter; trendy and sophisticated Miami, and the laid-back Florida Keys for great fishing, diving, and relaxation.

A Season for All

The southernmost of the continental states, Florida endures hot and humid summers. But the weather can be quite varied – Florida stretches through two US time zones (Eastern and Central) – and though South Florida rarely dips below 70°F (20°C), it can snow occasionally in Northeast Florida. Average summertime temperatures are in the low to mid-80s°F (high 20s°C), though they can rise into

Flamingos at Fort Lauderdale

the 90s°F (30s°C), especially in South Florida.

When to travel depends on what you plan to do. If you want to visit Orlando, the least crowded times are mid-January through mid-March and September through mid-November. The winter months are best for camping, with cooler weather and hibernating mosquitoes. Early fall and late spring are the best times of year for inexpensive beach vacations.

Culturally Cool

Florida is extremely culturally diverse. The state's earliest history intertwined Native Americans as well as settlers from Spain, England, France, Africa, the Caribbean, and South America, leaving a rich, multicultural legacy.

Florida's kinship with the American Deep South can be felt most in the north of the state, around Tallahassee and Pensacola, magnets for those moving from Georgia and Alabama. But from the time of its Spanish discovery, the state has always had a strong Latin flavor. Cuba is just 90 miles (145km) from Key West, a fact that has often affected Florida's history and still does. Cuban exiles and their progeny make up the largest contingent in Miami, lending color to the street life, spice to the cuisine, and an edge to the politics. The Hispanic population also includes Nicaraguans, Puerto Ricans, Colombians, Dominicans, and others from South and Central America. Other Caribbeans include Jamaicans, Bahamians, Haitians, and newcomers from Trinidad and Tobago.

Florida is a magnet, too, for the New Yorker. Accents in the supermarkets and around the swimming pools of Miami Beach and the Gold Coast are more likely to be laced with the heavy ironies of Brooklyn and Queens than the good-ol'-boy cheerfulness of the neighboring southern states of Georgia and Alabama. Italians, Greeks, Scandinavians running cruise lines, British visitors hungry for sunshine – think of a national group and you'll find it here.

The Florida Keys have always attracted a mixture of bohemians – artists, writers, and seekers after the good life flock here from all over America and beyond. This lively bunch of eccentrics defies any classification. Key West does have its own proud 'Conchs' named after the shellfish and (pronounced 'konks'). They trace their ancestry back to the American Revolution, when loyalists to the British crown fled to the Bahamas first and then on to the Keys, where their community still runs the scuba diving and charter fishing business and keeps aloof from 'interlopers'.

The Sunshine State is a truly unique melting pot, and its incredible diversity has created a vacation destination that welcomes visitors with open arms. Indeed, Floridians are some of the friendliest people you will meet anywhere.

Don CeSar Beach Resort, St Pete Beach

A BRIEF HISTORY

The flat peninsula of Florida emerged long ago from the sea, augmented by silt washed down by the mighty rivers of the north and coral reefs growing in the warm waters. In prehistoric times saber-toothed tigers prowled through the wetlands, while woolly mammoths, giant armadillos, and even tiny horses roamed the plains.

The first human beings arrived about 15,000 years ago, perhaps from farther north, but possibly from Central America. They lived by hunting and fishing, and especially from the generous supplies of shellfish. In South and Central Florida, in fact, some of the highest hills are the oyster-shell mounds piled up by these earliest inhabitants. Some of these mounds can still be seen, although many disappeared in mod-

An early map of Florida

ern times when the material they contained was used to make roads and tracks through the swamps.

Early Floridians had an easier life than most hunter-gatherers. Judging by surviving pieces, they had time to create artworks such as shell jewelry and beautiful statuettes. Ceremonial burials also suggest an organized religious life. Around 1450BC, they found that despite the infertile soil, the climate made it possible to cultivate crops such as maize, squash, cassava, and peppers. Archaeologists have recently dated systems of drainage canals to that period.

On the eve of the European discovery of the New World, Florida's indigenous population numbered tens of thousands, divided into five nations. Chief of these were the Timucua of the north, the Apalachee in the Panhandle, and the Calusa in the southwest.

European Discovery

Columbus was not far from Florida when he found the island of Hispaniola (now Haiti and the Dominican Republic) on his way to 'the Indies' in 1492. Other early explorers may have searched the Florida coast for a passage to the Pacific, but credit for Florida's discovery goes to Juan Ponce de

State Symbols

Florida has nearly two dozen official state symbols, everything from the state bird to the state beverage. If you know these, you may know as much, or more, than most locals. Animal: Florida panther. Drink: orange juice. Bird: mockingbird. Butterfly: zebra longwing. Flower: orange blossom. Freshwater fish: largemouth bass. Gem: moonstone. Marine mammal: manatee. Reptile: alligator. Saltwater fish: sailfish. Saltwater mammal: porpoise. Shell: horse conch. Stone: agatized coral. Tree: sabal palm. Wild flower: coreopsis.

León (1460–1521). Bored with life in Spain after the Moorish wars, he set out with Columbus on his second expedition in 1493. The voyage rekindled his taste for adventure, and by 1508 Ponce was on his way to Puerto Rico. He became the island's governor, but soon lost his position to the more influential Diego Columbus, son of the navigator.

In 1512, the Spanish king commissioned Ponce de León to find and explore the fabled 'Isle of Bimini'. The island, so legend said, concealed a spring with the miraculous power to restore youth to the aged. No doubt Ponce, 52 years old at the time, was inspired with hope. If it didn't work, there was still the prospect of gold and other provisions for his old age.

A 16th-century Spanish galleon

Setting sail for the Bahamas in search of Bimini, Ponce landed instead on the Florida coast, on April 2, 1513. From his first landfall, near present-day St Augustine, Ponce and his crew sailed down the coast, past Cape Canaveral, along the Keys, and out to Dry Tortugas. From there they continued north along the Gulf Coast to Charlotte Harbor before returning to Puerto Rico after an eight-month voyage. Ponce had missed Bimini, but found an immense land full of promise, which his grateful sovereign granted him the right to conquer, govern, and colonize. But conquering wasn't on the cards.

Blighted Hopes

Ponce's discovery was a bitter disappointment to him. On a second voyage to Florida in 1521 he took along two ships, 200 colonists, livestock, and farm implements. Though Ponce knew from his first visit that the Calusa Indians at Charlotte Harbor were hostile, he chose to land there anyway. His party was building shelters when warriors attacked. Ponce was badly wounded by an arrow and carried back to his ship. By the time the disillusioned settlers reached Cuba, their leader was near death. He was buried in Puerto Rico.

What's in a name?

Ponce de León named Florida after the date in his calendar, *Pascua Florida*, the Feast of the Flowers at Easter.

The pattern of great expectations and dashed hopes repeated itself in later ventures. Pánfilo de Narváez, a follower of Cortés, set out from Cuba in 1528 with 600 soldiers and colonists, but quickly lost 200 of his party in skirmishes. Marching inland from Tampa Bay, they expected to find food and water easily, but they almost starved. The fabled gold was nowhere to be found; the only inhabitants were Indian women and children living in mud huts. Panic-stricken in a strange and hostile land, Narváez and his followers built makeshift boats and set sail for Mexico, which they thought was near by. Of the 242 who manned the boats, only four reached Mexico City. Narváez was not among them. A search party sent out by Narváez's wife also disappeared.

Yet another ill-fated expedition was led by Hernando de Soto. Already rich and famous at the age of 36, the Spanish explorer left Cuba for Florida in 1538 with 600 optimistic volunteers. When they landed at Tampa Bay on May 30, 1539, they were met by Juan Ortiz, a survivor from the search party sent to find Narváez. Ortiz could now speak the Indian languages, and proved invaluable as a guide and interpreter. But this auspicious beginning was not followed by similar good fortune. Though de Soto's band marched as far as Kansas in search of riches, they found none. The farther they went, the more determined they became to continue until they discovered something, but they never did. Half of the men, including de Soto, died during the four-year odyssey. The survivors returned to Cuba empty-handed.

The First Permanent Settlement

Florida's east coast became strategically important as soon as Spanish treasure fleets began to follow the Gulf Stream along it. News that France was taking an interest drove Spain to found a colony. On September 8, 1565, Pedro Menéndez de Avilés and a detachment of soldiers arrived at the mouth of the St John's River, near present-day Jacksonville, where a party of French Huguenots had been struggling along in their small settlement at Fort Caroline.

The two great European nations were already engaged in a bitter contest for colonial domination, and a battle was certain. The French were caught by surprise, with their ships away at sea, and easily beaten. Later, the French fleet was wrecked on the coast in a storm, and the Spanish took in the survivors. Faced with the problem of what to do with the captives, Menéndez decided that the threat to his own party, and its limited food supply, was too great to ignore. Sparing women and children, Catholics, and musicians, he put the rest to the sword 'not as Frenchmen, but as Lutherans'.

About 30 miles (48km) south of Fort Caroline, Menéndez founded the first permanent settlement in North America, the

Castillo de San Marcos, St Augustine

colony of St Augustine. It suffered from sporadic Indian attacks and in 1586 was raided by the English pirate Sir Francis Drake. The difficulties of defending the outpost were plain, but it was judged essential, and in response to later English, Indian, and pirate assaults, the Spanish constructed a massive stone fortress, Castillo de San Marcos, which still stands today.

Imperial Rivals

When the King of France, Louis XIV, attempted to seat his grandson on the Spanish throne, England was quick to see the peril. Spain and France united could dictate to the rest of Europe and the world.

The War of the Spanish Succession in 1702 brought English forces deep into Florida. Though the fortress at St Augustine survived an eight-week siege and never fell, the English wiped out most of Spain's other military outposts and religious missions in four years of war.

With Spanish power in decline, England and France could concentrate on fighting for North America. The Seven Years War in Europe spread to the New World as the 'French and Indian War.' Despite Indian support, French forces went down in defeat, leaving the English as masters of the continent. In 1763 Florida was officially ceded to England.

With the new European overlords came a shift in population. Descendants of the original American Indians, shattered by European diseases, the slave trade, and internal feuds, left Florida with the Spanish to find more peaceful homes in the west and in Cuba. Their farms and villages were taken over by a mixture of tribes from Alabama and Georgia called the Seminoles (from the Spanish *cimarrones*, 'runaway' or 'wild').

The Seminoles were courted by English traders bearing pots, knives, guns, and axes. The government gave grants to organize plantations, and soon indigo, rice, turpentine, sugar, and oranges became lucrative exports.

Lost Colony

After the British defeat in the American War of Independence, Florida was returned to Spanish rule by the Treaty of Paris of 1783. But the allegiance of Florida's Seminole and European inhabitants remained with Britain. In a further bizarre turn of events, the British, now allied with Spain in the Napoleonic Wars, landed forces in western Florida in 1814, only to withdraw again when US troops, under future president Andrew Jackson, marched into the territory. Further American incursions marked this final, unhappy spell of Spanish rule. Unable to control Florida, Spain ceded it to the US in 1819. Jackson became its first US governor in 1821.

American settlers flooded into Florida, causing consternation among the long-time inhabitants. The Seminoles were pushed off the fertile lands of the north and into the Everglades. In 1830, Andrew Jackson, now president, signed an

Seminoles attacking an American fort, c.1837

Act of Congress ordering all American Indians to move to new lands in the frontier territories to the west. Some accepted; others stood and fought. In the Second Seminole War of 1835–42 it became clear that conventional US forces were unsuited to combating the hit-and-run tactics of opponents who could disappear into the steaming swamps of southern Florida. The Seminole leader Osceola was seized, although under a flag of truce, and died in prison not long after. His followers did not give up the struggle, but were forced deeper into the Everglades. The war ended in stalemate, but only a few hundred Seminoles remained, in scattered villages.

Civil War

With peace came prosperity, and, in 1845, statehood. There was a new wave of northern immigrants, but for the most part local power rested on plantation owners, who depended on slave labor. Thus Florida took the side of the South in the Civil War, seceding from the Union in 1861 and joining the Confederacy. But Union forces easily captured and occupied most of Florida's ports and forts. Many Confederate troops were sent to fight distant battles, and those who remained were mainly engaged in raiding supply lines.

With the war's end in 1865 came nominal freedom for the slaves, although many in fact continued to work for their former masters in scarcely better conditions. Their hopes for equal rights were dashed, and Florida acquired a corrupt, segregationist state government. However, the war had brought the state to the attention of northern investors.

Railroad Barons and Early Tourists

By the last quarter of the 19th century, a number of enterprising businessmen had seen the potential of the state's geography and climate. Henry Morrison Flagler and Henry Bradley Plant both possessed the kind of pioneering spirit that was the driving force of that expansionary era. They also had the money to turn their dreams into reality. Flagler's East Coast Railroad drove through swamp and jungle, to reach Miami in 1896 and eventually span the water to Key West. Henry Plant's lines to Tampa and beyond opened up central and western Florida.

Railroad baron H.M. Flagler

It didn't take long for the good news to spread, and soon tourists were descending in droves. Permanent settlers came, too: between 1870 and 1890, Florida's population doubled. So did the pressure on the land. It was State Governor Napoleon Bonaparte Broward who dug the first spadeful of earth in 1905 to begin a massive drainage program. Hundreds of miles of canals and dykes converted huge tracts of the Everglades into dry land. Hailed at the time, the effort is now looked upon as a disaster by conservationists.

The tourist boom became a near riot in the mid-1920s, when real-estate prices began to soar. Suddenly, thousands of Americans wanted to own a piece of Florida for vacations, retirement, or just as an investment. More than 2,000 people a day flooded into the state, and soon the railroads forbade any railcar to advertise Miami as its destination. Then a ship from up north carrying would-be Floridians sank in Biscayne Bay; a hurricane in 1926 wrought havoc in the Miami area; the bottom fell out of land prices, and with the onset of the Great Depression in 1929, the bonanza was over.

Steaming up the Ocklawaha River in the 19th century

World War II and After

Florida's economy didn't recover until the beginning of World War II, when thousands of recruits arrived at the state's bases. These soldiers fell under the same spell as others before them. When peace came, many returned to Florida to live. The state's economy diversified. Agriculture expanded to provide winter vegetables for the north and more fruit, especially citrus. Cattle farmers profited from cheap land prices in the interior. The 1959 revolution in Cuba brought an influx of 300,000 Cubans, swelling Miami's population.

Recent decades have seen the love affair with Florida continue. Airlines bring vacationers in greater numbers than ever. Winter sun-seekers drive down from frigid northern cities in just a couple of days.

Travel has yet another dimension in Florida: It was from Cape Canaveral that America first probed into space. Today, crowds flock to the 'Space Coast' to watch the shuttle launches.

Changing Patterns

When Walt Disney started to buy up land near Orlando in the late 1960s, he began a process that was to alter Florida tourism beyond recognition. There had long been a handful of purpose-built holiday 'attractions', but when Walt Disney World opened in 1971 it made them look insignificant. Now the Walt Disney World Resort is the most world's popular vacation destination. Other theme parks cluster around, and Orlando has turned from a market town to the city with more hotel rooms than any other in the United States except Las Vegas.

Splashdown on SeaWorld's Journey to Atlantis

European travelers find Miami and Orlando among America's most accessible cities. Refugees from the cold north and the Caribbean still arrive in their thousands. Spanish explorers sought gold and the fountain of youth. The objectives of today's visitors are not so different, except their fountain of youth is non-stop fun.

Historical Landmarks

1497 European explorers see Florida for the first time, and in 1502 it is depicted on a Spanish map as peninsula-like.

1513 In March, Ponce de León sees land, and in April, in the vicinity of present-day St Augustine, he names this land *Pascua Florida*, meaning 'the Feast of the Flowers at Easter'.

1565 In August, Pedro Menéndez de Avilés of Spain enters a harbor and calls it San Agustín, which becomes St Augustine.

1763 Florida is given to the British, as the Spanish swap it for Havana.

1783 Florida goes back to the Spanish.

1819 The Spanish relinquish Florida to the US.

1845 Florida is granted statehood on March 3.

1886 Henry M. Flagler buys the first transportation link in the chain of railroad and hotel properties, building down the East Coast to Key West.

1914 The world's first scheduled airline service begins from St Petersburg to Tampa on New Year's Day.

1950s After the invention of the air conditioner, Florida's population grows by 78 percent, making it the tenth-most populous state.

1958 *Explorer I*, the first earth satellite, is launched by the US as operations begin at Cape Canaveral by the National Aeronautics and Space Administration (NASA).

1959 Cubans fleeing Castro begin arriving in Miami.

1971 Walt Disney World opens near Orlando, Florida.

1982 Epcot opens as Disney's second park in Orlando.

1990 Universal Studios opens near Orlando, Florida.

2000 Florida gains international fame for its 'hanging chads' as George W. Bush narrowly defeats Al Gore in the presidential election.

2003 Space shuttle *Columbia* is destroyed upon re-entry to earth.

2004 Four hurricanes cause large-scale damage to the state.

2005 Space shuttle *Discovery* completes first shuttle mission in two years. Hurricane Wilma leaves 300,000 homes without electricity.

2008 A nationwide recession hits Florida hard, choking its job, real estate, and tourism industries.

WHERE TO GO

In terms of size, Florida is the fourth-most populated US state, and at more than 58,000 sq miles (150,000 sq km) it's the size of England and Wales combined. There's more than enough to see and do to keep you going for months, let alone the average two-week vacation. So you will have to make choices. The Gulf or the Atlantic Coast? Combined with Walt Disney World? Miami and the Keys as well? Or instead?

Most visitors rent a car. It's undoubtedly the best means of getting around. But beware, driving distances in Florida can be deceiving; the state stretches 832 miles (1,339km) from Pensacola in the Panhandle to Key West. A trip from Miami to Orlando, for instance, is five hours by car. But it's easy to find your way with a good map or navigation system.

We travel north from Miami and the Florida Keys up the Atlantic Coast through Fort Lauderdale, Palm Beach, and the 'Space Coast' to St Augustine. Then we visit Orlando and Central Florida, home of the Walt Disney World Resort, and several more theme parks, before going south to the Everglades. We then visit the fast-expanding resorts of the Gulf Coast, traveling from Naples to Tampa. Finally, we visit the Panhandle. But first comes a famous American vacation spot, which continues its exciting revival.

SOUTHEAST FLORIDA

Miami Beach

The city of **Miami Beach**, 'where the sun spends the winter,' is in fact a narrow 7-mile (11km) strip of land separated from mainland Miami by Biscayne Bay and connected to it by causeways. It's here that you'll find something of the opu-

Stylish and safe on Miami's fashionable South Beach

lence and brash taste that have become as much a part of American legend as the Wild West.

Collins Avenue, the north–south spine of the island, is lined by hotels and holiday apartments. The resort's heyday was in the 1950s, when vast pleasure palaces aspired to be the biggest and most luxurious; 20 years later it was no longer fashionable. In recent years, revitalization efforts and building renovations have caused the area to blossom again. A new generation – upscale 20- and 30-somethings – has popularized the avenue. Hotels have had face-lifts, and still try to outdo each other in high season, but, except in high season, the competition mainly takes the form of offering special rates.

In contrast are the more modest Art Deco hotels and self-service apartments of **South Beach**, an area developed in the 1930s that has experienced a similar rebirth. The seafront along **Ocean Drive** benefits from a wide strip of parkland, and, between about 10th and 13th streets, it has become a trendy place to be seen. Real or would-be models and other 'beautiful people' parade at the open-air bars, while bikers and skaters cut in and out of the sunset traffic snarl.

One block west of Collins Avenue, on Park Avenue, is the **Bass Museum of Art** (Tue–Sat 10am–5pm, Sun 11am–5pm; charge). Its collection spans more than 500 years and four continents, including European masters, 20th-century paintings, sculpture, and photography from North America, Latin America and the Caribbean. The museum also hosts temporary exhibitions.

Just north of South Beach is the pedestrianized **Lincoln Road Mall**, Miami's trendiest shopping street, with boutiques, stylish shops, and cafés. Above Arthur Godfrey Boulevard are the top-of-the-line hotels, including the legendary **Fontainebleau Miami Beach**. The 'Fount'n-Blue,' as it's usually pronounced, was built in 1954 to attract high rollers and movie stars and has been recently modernized to keep the celebrities coming. Today it's a 37-story, all-suite resort offering visitors breathtaking views of the beach, as well as

The Art Deco District

Thanks to the extraordinary number of buildings in the 'streamlined, modern' style, 1 sq mile (2.6 sq km) of Miami Beach known as the **Art Deco District** has been declared a national preservation zone. Nowhere else in America is there such a concentration of architecture from the 1930s and early 1940s. Hotels and apartments were built at modest cost using cast concrete and stucco, decorated with chrome, stainless steel, glass blocks, and plastics. Thumbing its nose at the Depression, the flashy style set out to attract a new generation of middle-class tourists. The Miami Design Preservation League organizes guided tours of this unique quarter (tel: 305-672-2014). If you walk it on your own, stroll along Ocean Drive between 5th and 15th streets and the neighboring blocks to the west.

heated pools (including one on the 7th floor), waterfalls, hidden bars, shops, and golf.

The Miami Beach **boardwalk** begins at 21st Street and rambles between hotels and the beach as far as 46th Street. The beach is wide and flat, but not especially attractive, and is difficult to reach in places. Too often private property bars the way, and there are few points of access. At 74th Street you'll find more modest hotels and a small-town feeling.

North of Miami Beach

Leading north from Miami Beach along the string of offshore islands, Route A1A winds through the pleasant resort of **Surfside** (at about 93rd Street) and then on to **Bal Harbour**, with its waffle-faced condominiums and elegant hotels. Don't miss Bal Harbour Shops, a luxury mall renowned as much for its setting as for its merchandise.

Farther along A1A, **Haulover Park** is sandwiched between the bay and the ocean. On the bay side, Haulover Marina has berths for fishing boats and is the starting point for cruises along the Intracoastal Waterway to Fort Lauderdale. The park's ocean side has a beach with picnic places.

Around 196th Street, **Aventura** is famous for its exclusive golf and tennis resorts, and for a shopping mall, **Aventura Mall**, that is vast even by local standards. The resorts continue in an unbroken line to the north, but at this point we turn back to Florida's sprawling metropolis.

Miami

Its Spanish-speaking culture has made Miami more a South American hub than a North American city. Before Miami became the fast-moving Mecca it is today, it was a quiet village – that is until magnate Henry Flagler was persuaded to extend his railroad south in 1896. Now the metropolitan population is more than 2.4 million, and the suburbs stretch for

30 miles (50km). Some neighborhoods are on their way up, others are run-down, and some are definitely 'no-go' areas.

The Metrorail brings people from the suburbs into the city center, while the automated Metromover makes a loop round the downtown district. A ride on the latter is primarily for fun; there is not much in the way of views, as the system doesn't cover much ground. It was built as part of a renewal program for downtown Miami, which is certainly livelier than it was in the 1970s, although the shops are mostly of the fast-buck variety: cheap luggage and discount electronics.

The post modernist **Miami-Dade Cultural Center** (101 West Flagler Street) was designed by Philip Johnson and contains an art museum, auditorium, library, and history museum. The **Miami Art Museum** (Tue–Fri 10am–5pm, Sat–Sun noon–5pm; charge; www.miamiartmuseum.org) has a sculpture court, hosts temporary exhibitions and has a strong collection

The sun sets on Downtown Miami's commercial center

of post-war American art. The **Historical Museum of Southern Florida** (Mon–Sat 10am–5pm, Sun noon–5pm; charge; www.hmsf.org) features dozens of hands-on displays that explore the region's history, archaeology, and cultural mix.

Flagler Street meets **Biscayne Boulevard** and the bay at **Bayfront Park**. The big draw here is **Bayside Marketplace**, a waterfront complex of shops and restaurants with a pier, yacht berths, promenade, and free entertainment. North across a drawbridge is the **Port of Miami**, home to sleek cruise ships that sail to the Caribbean.

While **Little Havana** begins in downtown Miami, the center of the district is a 30-block section stretching west along SW 8th Street called **Calle Ocho**. Restaurants here specialize in Cuban cuisine and street-side stands serve *café cubano*. Lots of small businesses flourish in the area, too, such as **El Credito Cigar Factory**, where you are welcome to watch the cigar-rollers at work.

Just off MacArthur Causeway, about midway between the airport and South Beach, **Parrot Jungle Island** (daily 10am–6pm; charge; www.parrotjungle.com) houses macaws, flamingos, and other exotic birds in seemingly unrestricted freedom. Parrots eat out of your hand – you can feed them with seed dispensed at the park. The **Miami Children's Museum** (daily 10am–6pm; charge; www.miamichildrensmuseum.org) across MacArthur Causeway from Parrot Jungle, offers galleries of interactive exhibits where your heirs can frolic in sand castles, learn about finances in a 6ft (1.8m) piggy bank, and discover nutrition tips.

Orientation point

In Miami, Flagler Street, the main east–west artery, is the 'zero' for street numbers. Streets run east–west; avenues run north–south with Miami Avenue as the 'zero.' In the four quadrants thus created, streets and avenues are labeled NE, SE, SW, and NW.

A talented dolphin show at the legendary Seaquarium

Key Biscayne

One of the earliest marine parks, the **Seaquarium** (daily 9.30am–6pm; charge; www.miamiseaquarium.com) is reached by the Rickenbacker Causeway, 'the steepest hill in Miami,' which arcs over the bay to the island of Key Biscayne. Compared with SeaWorld *(see page 68)*, it is showing its age, but it has introduced a swim-with-the-dolphin program to keep up with the times. Shows include shark-feeding, juggling sea lions, leaping killer whales, and basketball-playing dolphins, the 'Miami Heatwave,' not to be confused with the local human team, the Miami Heat.

The northern part of Key Biscayne is given over to **Crandon Park**, a vast public beach with facilities. Don't pick the sea oats that line the beach; they prevent erosion of the sand.

At the southern end is **Bill Baggs Cape Florida State Park**, site of the 1825 Cape Florida lighthouse, which is open to visitors.

The 'Gables' and the 'Grove'

Southwest of the city center, the wealthy community of **Coral Gables** is graced with fountains, gardens, and Spanish architecture. The excellent **Lowe Art Museum** (Tue–Wed and Fri–Sat 10am–5pm, Thur noon–7pm, Sun noon–5pm; charge; www.lowemuseum.org) on the University of Miami campus (1301 Stanford Drive) has collections of primitive and Native American art, 17th-century Spanish paintings, and 20th-century art, especially sculpture. South on Old Cutler Road, the lush **Fairchild Tropical Botanical Garden** (daily 9.30am–4.30pm; charge; www.fairchildgarden.org) comprises more than 80 acres (32 hectares) of tropical plants, trees, shrubs, and flowers. Tram tours can take you round, or you can explore on foot.

The Spanish-style Congregational Church in Coral Gables

Coconut Grove is a lively village-cum-suburb on the shores of the bay, with cozy little shops, bikeways, open-air cafés, clubs, and live theater. It dates back to the years before Miami existed – a few early buildings still survive, notably the 19th-century **Barnacle**, built from timber salvaged from shipwrecks. The area's main focus is the **Gallery at Cocowalk**, a two-level mall in the middle of the Grove with shops, restaurants, and cinemas. The place is packed most nights, but that's part of the attraction.

Don't stray too far to the west of the Grove, a notoriously dangerous area.

Located at the Miami end of Coconut Grove is the Italianate palace of **Vizcaya** (Vizcaya Museum and Gardens; daily 9.30am–4.30pm; charge; www.vizcayamuseum.com), built in 1916 for the tractor magnate James Deering. An odd mix of styles, it is decorated with tapestries, massive furniture, and classical sculpture. Outside, elegant terraces sweep down to the shores of

Elegant, eccentric Vizcaya

Biscayne Bay, but the estate's grounds also include tracts of dense jungle, left uncut at Deering's insistence.

Across South Miami Avenue, the **Miami Museum of Science** (daily 10am–6pm; charge; www.miamisci.org) features dozens of hands-on exhibits, while the adjacent **Planetarium** screens shows on various aspects of astronomy. The adjoining wildlife center provides a home for injured birds of prey.

South of the City

The cageless **Metrozoo** (daily 9.30am–5.30pm; charge; www.miamimetrozoo.com), south at 12400 SW 152nd Street, is one of the largest and most modern zoos in the United States, home to white Bengal tigers, gorillas, giraffes, and elephants. One of the main attractions is Dr. Wilde's World, an indoor gallery that showcases permanent, seasonal, and traveling exhibits featuring varied topics, regions of the world and cultures. There is also a spectacular walk-through aviary.

Monkey Jungle (daily 9.30am–5pm; charge), an hour's

Parrott fashion in
Monkey Jungle

drive south of Miami, keeps human visitors caged while 500 other primates are free to swing around in the cultivated tropical jungle.

Biscayne National Park (daily 7am–5.30pm; charge) offers snorkeling, diving, and swimming over shipwrecks and coral reefs. The park is home to the world's third-longest-living coral reef. From Convoy Point near Homestead, glass-bottomed boats take visitors on three-hour excursions over the reefs.

HEADING SOUTH: THE FLORIDA KEYS

Curving westward from below Miami, a 120-mile (190km) long chain of islands called the Florida Keys is stitched together by 43 bridges. First built as the last stage of Flagler's East Coast Railroad, the **Overseas Highway** now allows drivers to leapfrog out to the bohemian retreat of Key West.

South from Homestead follow Highway 1, or take the quieter Card Sound Road, through 30 miles (50km) of swampland. You'll soon be on **Key Largo**, the largest of the islands. Its southern end is a ribbon of uninspired commercial development, but is the base for trips to the **John Pennekamp Coral Reef State Park** (daily 8am–5pm; charge; www.pennekamppark.com), 27 miles (43km) of coral reefs and tropical fish. Plenty of shops rent diving equipment, cameras, and boats. To scuba dive you need to be certified, but there are schools here where you can sign up and pay tuition for lessons. Glass-bottomed boats also make regular trips along this spectacularly colored reef for those who prefer to keep dry while admiring the fish.

Farther down the Keys at **Islamorada**, you'll find plenty of opportunities for diving and snorkeling, as well as fishing for some 600 species of fish in the self-proclaimed 'sport-fishing' capital of the world. At one of the oldest marine shows in Florida, **Theater of the Sea** (daily 9.30am–5pm; charge; www. theaterofthesea.com), trainers lead visitors from one pool to another, pointing out dolphins, rays, sharks, and sea lions.

Fun with Flipper

The **Dolphin Research Center** (daily 9am–4.30pm; charge; www.dolphins.org) on Grassy Key offers one of Florida's best and least commercialized swim-with-the-dolphin programs. The center has a range of options, including some designed

Get away from it all at Islamorada

for amputees or guests who suffer from emotional and mental conditions such as autism.

Marathon, chief town of the Middle Keys, is a sizable resort and a diving and fishing center. Its museum is informative on the geology of the Keys and their early inhabitants. After Marathon, Flagler's engineers met their biggest challenge: 7 miles (11km) of sea to be bridged on the way to the Lower Keys. The **Seven-Mile Bridge** still stands, a monument to the hundreds of workers who died during its construction between 1905 and 1912. Now it's defunct (except for fishing), replaced by a new road bridge with parapets frustratingly blocking the view. Stop at either end to see the bridges sweep over turquoise water into the misty distance.

Bahia Honda State Park (daily 8am–5pm; charge), a state nature reserve, has a tropical sandy beach, something of a rarity in the Keys. You'll notice the strange double-decker bridge here: The road used to be on top.

At last Highway 1, which follows the entire East Coast for 2,000 miles (3,200km), can go no farther; you've reached the remote town of Key West.

Conch Republic

Key West natives and long-time residents call themselves Conchs (pronounced 'konks'), a name taken from a hard-shelled (and some would argue hard-headed) sea creature that frequents these parts. Those who live here dislike being pushed around, and at times go to excesses to prove it. In 1982, for example, they bristled when the Border Patrol set up a roadblock across the Overseas Highway to catch drug runners and made all who tried to pass prove they were US citizens. Outraged, locals fired a cannon, declared themselves to be the "Conch Republic" and demanded $1 billion in foreign aid. President Ronald Reagan politely declined, but townspeople made their point.

Set sail from Key West's historical marina

Key West

The word 'key' comes from the Spanish *cayo*, meaning a small island. It is possible that **Key West** was named *Cayo Oeste* by Ponce de León. But for many years it was called *Cayo Hueso* (Bone Island), perhaps because Indian battles in the 18th century left the island littered with them. Pirates and wreckers were the main inhabitants until the US Navy came to plant the flag in 1822. But for all its violent past, Key West is one of the friendliest towns in Florida.

Four hours' drive from Miami, the tiny subtropical island is actually nearer to Havana. Its population comprises retirees, Cuban exiles, hay fever sufferers who find the pure air here a boon, descendants of the original Conchs who came from the Bahamas, writers, painters, and a large gay community. Now they all claim to be Conchs *(see box opposite)*. You approach the island via the newer, commercial quarter. Follow the road to the old town.

Sloppy Joe's

The Sloppy Joe's bar that Ernest Hemingway used to frequent is now called Capt. Tony's and is around the corner from the current Sloppy Joe's, on Greene Street.

In **Duval Street**, lined with shops selling arts and crafts, souvenirs, and T-shirts, **Sloppy Joe's** (daily 9am–2am) is one of the noisiest of several bars. Duval Street ends at **Old Mallory Square**, scene of a nightly free show. Toward sunset, a crowd gathers on this stone quay to be entertained by musicians, jugglers, fire-eaters, and others.

Close by Mallory Square stands the terminal of the **Conch Tour Train**, a mock railway engine pulling buggies on a 14-mile (23km) trip past the island's sights. The Old Town Trolley company competes with it, and trishaws carry sightseers on shorter trips.

The **Ernest Hemingway Home and Museum** (907 Whitehead Street; daily 9am–5pm; charge; www.hemingway home.com), set in a tropical garden, was owned by the author for 30 years, although he lived here for only about 10 of them. But some of his most famous books, including *For Whom the Bell Tolls* and *A Farewell to Arms*, were at least partly written in Key West, though *To Have and Have Not* is his only novel set in the town. A climb up the lighthouse opposite is worth it for the view.

The famous painter and naturalist John James Audubon came to Key West in 1832 to paint the birds of the Florida Keys. The so-called **Audubon House** (daily 9.30am–5pm; charge; www.audubonhouse.com) has some good English furniture, but only a tenuous connection with the man himself.

On Front Street, the **Mel Fisher Maritime Heritage Museum** (daily 9.30am–5pm; charge; www.melfisher.org) displays finds from the *Nuestra Señora de Atocha*, one of eight Spanish galleons wrecked off this coast in 1622. After

Posing at Southernmost Point

years of searching, Fisher found the treasure, valued at hundreds of millions of dollars, in 1985.

Stroll through the Truman Annex, an attractive redevelopment of former naval housing, to see the immaculately restored **Truman Little White House** (daily 9am–5pm; charge), favorite retreat of President Harry S. Truman in the 1940s and '50s. **City Cemetery** (daily sunrise–6pm; tour charge; tel: 305-393-8177) is littered with humorous epitaphs. Near by, there's not much left of **Fort Zachary Taylor**, but the beach is one of the best in the area. The intense sunshine here can be a problem, so take precautions against overexposure even when walking the city streets. The **coral reef** offshore breaks the waves, creating a haven for snorkelers.

About a mile (1.6km) south of the end of Highway 1, at the farthest tip of Key West, a monument shaped like a buoy marks the **Southernmost Point** of the United States. The Cuban coast is just 90 miles (145km) away from here to the south.

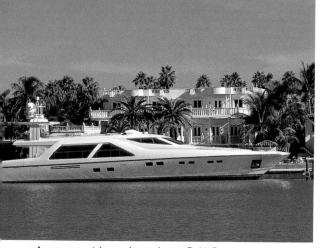

A common sight on the exclusive Gold Coast

HEADING NORTH: THE GOLD COAST

Several roads lead north from Miami along this celebrated 70-mile (112km) stretch of Atlantic coastline, named for its golden sand as well as its incredible wealth. The older highway, US 1, lies just inland from the coast; then comes I-95, the multi-lane Interstate, the best option if you want to travel fast; the Florida Turnpike toll road and US 441 run farther inland than the others. Nearest to the sea is route A1A. For much of the way A1A links the barrier islands – there are some fabulous views along the way, but it can be slow going.

This coastline includes half a dozen of Florida's most famous winter resorts. At first glance it's difficult to distinguish one place from another, but they all have enough individuality to inspire loyalty in their many visitors.

The first, rather quiet, resorts north of Miami are **Hallandale** and **Hollywood**; the latter is best known for the Seminole Reservation, home to the huge Seminole Hard Rock Hotel and Casino. **Dania**, northwest of Hollywood, is known locally as one of the antiques capitals of Florida; all along US 1 dealers have set up shops in the sunshine. And in nearby **Sunrise**, you'll find **Sawgrass Mills**, the world's largest outlet mall, with more than 350 stores plus cinemas and restaurants. Just about every retailer you can imagine has a discount place here.

Fort Lauderdale

Fort Lauderdale straddles more than 300 miles (420km) of navigable inland waterways lined with over 30,000 private boats and yachts. Most hotels and many motels face the beach, separated from it by the coast road. For an evening visit you can park in sight of the waves and make forays to restaurants across the highway. During the day old Fort Lauderdale and the Bennet House Museum make interesting diversions.

The best way to see the town is to take a ride on one of the sightseeing 'trams.' Guides provide commentary as the tour passes sumptuous waterfront homes, orange groves, the car museum, and the **International Swimming Hall of Fame** (daily 9am–5pm; charge; www.ishof.org).

On SE 17th Street, the misleadingly named Port Everglades is a major terminal for cruise ships and freighters. All sorts of **excursion cruises** start from Fort Lauderdale, some going as far as the Bahamas. Mississippi-River-style paddleboats take regular daytime trips to the mangrove swamps and dinner cruises along the Intracoastal Waterway.

North from Fort Lauderdale, **Pompano Beach** is lined with towering condominiums, and is well known for the harness races held at Pompano Park. The beach is quieter at **Boca Raton**, where as many people fish from the shore as take to the water. Boca claims to be the 'Winter Polo Capital of the World,' but for mere financial mortals, the town's fine **Museum of Art** (www.bocamuseum.org) is the main attraction.

Palm Beach

At **Palm Beach**, one of America's wealthiest communities, beautiful Italianate homes are half hidden behind walls and sculptured hedges. Some of the houses crowded along the 5-mile (8km) strip of land are used for only a few weeks each winter. Drive along A1A to admire the landscape gardening and see how the rich arrange things when they get the chance. From Christmas through February it's very crowded; at other times Palm Beach can be very quiet. The beach itself is narrow, since storms have eroded much of it. **Worth Avenue**, set amid Mediterranean-style buildings from the 1920s and palm-filled courtyards, houses elegant shops and restaurants. It all makes Beverly Hills's Rodeo Drive look comparatively downmarket.

Norton Museum of Art

The **Henry Morrison Flagler Museum** (Tue–Sat 10am–5pm, Sun noon–5pm; charge; www.flaglermuseum.us) on Coconut Row, formerly the rail tycoon's extravagant 1902 mansion known as 'Whitehall,' retains much of its original, luxurious furniture and photos. Flagler's own private railway carriage is parked in the garden, complete with cast-iron stove and copper-lined shower.

Just across the causeway, **West Palm Beach** has the motels, light industry, and international airport that its upscale neighbor wasn't prepared to accommodate. The **Norton Museum of Art** on US 1 (1451 S. Olive Avenue; Mon–Sat 10am–5pm, Sun 1–5pm, May–Oct closed Mon; charge; www.nortonmuseum. org) has a splendid collection of French Impressionists and post-Impressionists.

At the Lion Country Safari

From West Palm Beach, the causeway at Blue Heron Boulevard leads across to Palm Beach Shores, a hotel and motel development. Inland at **Lion Country Safari** (daily 9.30am–4.30pm; charge; www.lioncountrysafari.com) you can drive through herds of elephants and zebras, past lions and ostriches, but if you come in a convertible, you'll have to swap it for one of the park's cars.

The area labeled the Gold Coast ends at West Palm Beach. Under different names (Treasure Coast, Space Coast, and First Coast), the Florida beaches continue for another 300 miles (480km) north to the state border. **Treasure Coast** acquired its name from the Spanish ships that were wrecked along it, spilling their cargoes of gold and silver. But truth to tell, any part of Florida's Atlantic seaboard could make the same claim. Once a mangrove swamp with offshore sandbars, much of it is a long string of islands separated from the mainland by a saltwater strip called Indian River or Indian Creek. The leisurely route A1A connects the islands and resorts, frequently crossing bridges where inlets link the ocean to the Indian River.

The **Jonathan Dickinson State Park** (daily 8am–sundown; charge), 13 miles (20km) south of Stuart, provides vacation cabins, hook-ups for campers, and facilities for fishing, swimming, boating, canoeing, and hiking.

CENTRAL EAST FLORIDA: THE SPACE COAST

Cape Canaveral

A nature reserve with alligators, eagles, and armadillos shares **Merritt Island** with scented orange groves and NASA (the National Aeronautics and Space Administration).

From Cape Canaveral, the United States began to send rockets into space in the 1950s. Near by, the **John F. Kennedy Space Center** (daily except launch days 9am–6pm; charge; www.kennedyspacecenter.com) has been the launch site for American manned explorations of space, including the first mission to land a man on the moon in 1969. Now it's the base of the space shuttles. To find out when the next take-off is scheduled, visit the website, check the daily papers, or call 321-449-4444. Whether there's a launch or not, it's well worth visiting the Kennedy Space Center Visitor Complex,

Watching a launch is the experience of a lifetime

just off NASA Causeway linking A1A and US 1. Expect to spend at least half a day. In addition to the tours to the space shuttle launch pads and the Apollo/Saturn V Center, there are multimedia shows, a shuttle launch simulator, hands-on displays, and an IMAX cinema. Near by, but with its own admission charge, is the **Astronaut Hall of Fame**, with its Simulator Station interactive area featuring a variety of astronaut-training devices.

> ### Spce pioneer
>
> Man's passion for space travel got a real lift when Alan B. Shepard Jr. became the first American and second human in space on May 5, 1961. He was one of the original seven Mercury astronauts, true space pioneers who often flew in capsules that amounted to little more than oversize tin cans.

East of the spaceport, Port Canaveral is the newest of Florida's cruise terminals. If your holiday combines the **Walt Disney World Resort** *(see page 51)* with a cruise on the *Disney Magic* or the *Disney Wonder* (www.disneycruise. com), your ship will leave from here.

Cocoa Beach, on the narrow island to the south, was tiny when the first astronauts came here to relax from their training. Now it's a growing resort, a favorite among surfers and teenagers who jam its sands near the old wooden pier. Its dunes are a great vantage point for watching space launches.

Daytona
Just north is the 'World's Most Famous Beach,' as **Daytona Beach** proudly proclaims itself. Its 23 miles (37km) of hard-packed sand double as a roadway for a $5 toll. The 10mph (16km/h) speed limit hardly recalls the roaring twenties and thirties when Sir Henry Segrave and Sir Malcolm Campbell set world land-speed records here, culminating in Campbell's 276mph (444km/h) in 1935.

The flat sands, lifeguard towers, and shallow water make the beach safe for children, so long as they remember to dodge the traffic. And, like every Florida beach, it's at its best at dawn, when joggers scarcely bother the myriad seabirds and waders. However, beware of rip currents.

Each year, the 400-mile (645km) Daytona 500 stock-car race is held at the **Daytona International Speedway** (www.daytonainternationalspeedway.com). The event is usually scheduled for late February. An entire car and motorcycle culture has grown up around the track, with parades, flea markets, and special events. Hot-rodders and bikers in black leather cruise the streets and 'burn rubber' at the traffic lights. Interactive **Daytona 500 Experience** (daily 9am–7pm; charge) is the other big draw at the speedway, an attraction with live shows, two theaters, and dozens of interactive activities that put racing car enthusiasts in the driver's seat. You can also tour the speedway.

Inland Excursions

A trip to Lake George and Ocala National Forest is worth the drive westwards from Ormond Beach. Off Highway 40 at Juniper Springs, warm clear water surges from the ground to form a natural swimming pool. There are other crystal-clear springs, notably Alexander Springs in Ocala National Forest and **Silver Springs** (daily 10am–5pm; charge; www.silversprings.com) on its western edge. Here you can view a menagerie of animals from a safari boat, or spot fish and underwater plants through the floor of a glass-bottomed boat. Elsewhere on the grounds are a large bear exhibit, alligator feedings, and other animal exhibitions.

Route 19 through the **Ocala National Forest**, itself a sizable wilderness of lakes, hills, and springs, offers first-class camping, hiking, and fishing. To the west is the town of Ocala and its large horse industry, and, 35 miles (56km) to the northwest, the university city of Gainesville.

Oldest wooden schoolhouse in the United States, St Augustine

NORTHEAST FLORIDA

You'll come to shrug off superlatives in Florida, but **St Augustine** really *is* the oldest continuously settled city in the United States (founded in 1565, long before the *Mayflower* arrived). Its Spanish architecture, churches, and distinctly colonial atmosphere make it unlike anywhere else in Florida.

Most striking of the buildings is the **Castillo de San Marcos** (daily 8.45am–5.15pm; charge), a star-shaped Spanish fortress started in 1672 as a response to repeated raids by pirates and the English (in some cases there was no clear distinction between the two categories). Completed in 1695, its fortified walls, up to 12ft (3.7m) thick in places, are built of *coquina*, a stone formed of naturally bonded seashells and so effective at absorbing bombardment that the fortress never fell to assault. Exhibits and recreations of the historical events connected with the fort are presented daily.

A sightseeing trolley will take you on a tour of the historic old city, and then you can return to landmarks such as the well-restored **Oldest House** or the **Oldest Store Museum** (daily 9am–5pm; charge). This turn-of-the-20th-century emporium is stocked with 100,000 authentic items, many of them accidentally discovered in a warehouse attic. You can see old buttoned shoes and lace corsets, toys, groceries, medicines, bonnets, bicycles, hats, and guns.

Henry Flagler built the imposing Ponce de León Hotel for the new wave of tourists when his railroad reached St Augustine in 1888. Now it houses Flagler College. If you can, take a look inside the rotunda, the former hotel lobby. Across the street, another Flagler hotel is now the **Lightner Museum** (daily 9am–5pm; charge), a collection of Victoriana, Tiffany glass, and 19th-century musical instruments. A third former hotel on the square makes an impressive City Hall. Throughout the oldest sections of the city, artists and craft workers in authentic costumes create works using centuries-old techniques.

ORLANDO

Orlando entered the tourism business in a big way when Walt Disney World moved in down the road. The huge number of hotel rooms in the area, some 120,000, now means that Orlando can accommodate the biggest conventions and sports events, and Central Florida offers the world's greatest collection of purpose-built attractions, with **Walt Disney World**, **Universal Orlando** and **SeaWorld Orlando**.

Downtown Orlando

Many visitors to the area stay at or near Walt Disney World Resort or on International Drive and never venture into downtown Orlando, which is a pity. The downtown has been there much longer than the surrounding theme parks, so there is a wealth of local history and culture to be found in the numerous museums, art galleries, and small-scale tourist attractions. The **Orange County Regional History Center** (65 East Central Boulevard; Mon–Sat 10am–5pm, Sun noon–5pm; charge), easy to overlook, is rich in Central Florida's regional history. Displays here honor the Seminole Indians, the Cracker cowboys, citrus growers, 'Tin Can' tourists and, of course, Walt Disney himself.

The **Orlando Museum of Art** (Tue–Fri 10am–4pm, Sat–Sun noon–4pm, closed on major holidays; charge; www.omart.org) has a fine collection of art and photographs by the likes of Georgia O'Keeffe and Ansel Adams. Explorations of Mars and the human body are the exhibits at the **Orlando Science Center** (daily 10am–6pm, Fri–Sat until 9pm; charge; www.osc.org), which also offers a dinosaur excavation site and a miniature town.

Office buildings, downtown Orlando

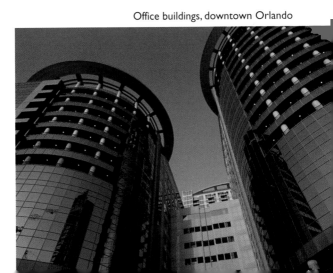

I-Drive and Kissimmee

International Drive, 12 miles (19km) away and as far again from Disney, grew from nothing in just a few years. It's a glitzy strip of hotels, restaurants, bars, and smaller attractions. **Wet'n'Wild** (6200 I-Drive; daily 10am–5pm or later; charge; www.wetnwild.com) is a great place to cool down. Don't miss the bizarre artefacts of **Ripley's Believe It or Not Odditorium**, housed in one of I-Drive's most memorable buildings. At the south end of I-Drive is **Pointe Orlando**, with upscale shopping, restaurants, more attractions, and cinemas.

In the years before Disney, **Kissimmee** was a sleepy town where the local cattle ranchers might drop in once a week. Now it's hard to find the old center amid miles of hotels, motels, factory outlets, and pubs. If you persist, you'll find it along Main Street and Broadway, where nothing much has changed. The town still holds a cattle market, and a rodeo twice a year.

The west side of town has followed Disney into the attractions culture. Highlights include taking one of **Forever Florida**'s horseback or swamp-buggy eco-safaris (daily 10am and 1pm; charge) and the rousing jousting at the **Medieval Times** dinner show (daily, hours vary; charge; www.medievaltimes.com).

Walt Disney World Resort

Tens of millions of people come every year to **Walt Disney World Resort** (www.disneyworld.com), one of the most popular tourist attractions on earth, lying 20 miles (32km) southwest of Orlando off I-4 and US 192. It's not just one theme park, but four, and an immense holiday resort with hotels, a campground, award-winning golf courses, water parks, tennis courts, vacation villas, shops, and nightclubs. Statistics show that 80 percent of all the visitors are adults, although for the purposes of Disney ticket sales, adulthood begins at the age of 10. Disney World Resort has even become America's favorite honeymoon destination. In all, the site covers some 28,000 acres (11,000 hectares), roughly twice the area of Manhattan Island.

Visitors to Walt Disney World Resort divide their time among four theme parks – the **Magic Kingdom**, **Disney's Hollywood Studios**, **Epcot**, and **Disney's Animal Kingdom** (daily 9am–6pm or later; charge). A day for each is hardly enough; if you stay longer, there are still more major attractions within the Disney area, including Blizzard Beach and Typhoon Lagoon (water adventure parks) and Downtown Disney (shopping, bars, and nightclubs). To encourage you, there are money-saving multi-day passes. These passes may seem expensive, but, once inside, all rides and attractions are free. Several tour companies offer packages – travel agents can give you full details of what's available.

Magic Kingdom visitor

The Magic Kingdom

From the Ticket and Transportation Center, take the sleek monorail or a ferryboat across the lake. If you've arrived by bus from a Disney hotel you'll be dropped off at the entrance. The Magic Kingdom is divided into seven different 'lands.' Stroll from one to the next, but not too slowly – there's a lot to see and do in the Magic Kingdom.

Main Street USA. Just beyond the entrance, you pass beneath Main Street Railroad Station into Town Square. **City Hall**, to your left, is the place for information about any as-

---

Theme Park Tips

If you have only one day, it will be hard to choose a park. Disney's Magic Kingdom certainly rules if you are a fairy-tale fan, as Animal Kingdom does for all who cherish nature's beasts. It's hard to top Universal's Islands of Adventure if you are a thrill-junkie, while Sea-World is a magnet for fans of marine life. Whatever your choice, here are a few tips to keep you safe and sane while getting the most for your money:

• Arrive early. That means getting to the parks at least 30 minutes before opening and heading straight for your favorite ride or show.

• Pace yourself. The parks are difficult to do in a single day because they are so huge. It's better to limit yourself to your top four or five attractions than to do them all and wear yourself into exhaustion.

• Pay attention to ride restrictions. Some have minimum heights, so if you have youngsters in tow they may not be admitted to some rides. Some also are not advisable for those with heart or back problems, pregnant women or people prone to motion sickness.

• Duck the crowds. Plan a visit when the masses are home. That means visiting from mid-September to mid-November and mid-January to mid-April. Summer is the worst time to come.

• Remember to be weather wise. If you are coming from late spring through mid fall, Florida's sun can cause a nasty burn or even the more dangerous sunstroke. When going outdoors, remember to use a 25 or higher-rated sunscreen. This is doubly important for those with fair skin.

• Reservations are a smart idea, especially during summer and holiday periods. Virtually all hotels and most restaurants take them.

pect of Walt Disney World Resort. The square is filled with life, and sometimes a crowd clusters round one of the Disney characters; they'll sign autographs but they don't speak.

Ahead of you, buildings in early 20th-century style line the street. Soon you'll see an antique double-decker bus or horse-drawn tram. You'll want to stop at the shops, but save that for the end of the day.

At the end of the street and across a bridge, a circular **Plaza** is backed by **Cinderella Castle**, the pinnacled symbol of the Magic Kingdom and home to the nightly 'Wishes' fireworks display. Radial routes lead from here to all the 'lands.' Our description proceeds clockwise.

Adventureland. The giant Banyan tree which supports the **Swiss Family Treehouse** is the first thing you'll spot. For all its woody appearance, it's actually made of concrete and vinyl. Just beyond, you can board boats for the **Jungle Cruise** or join **Pirates of the Caribbean** for a voyage to their treasure trove via some spirited animatronics.

Cinderella Castle

Frontierland. This land celebrates America's Old West, both real and legendary. Take aim at the old-time Shootin' Gallery, go for a roller-coaster ride through Gold Rush days on the **Big Thunder Mountain Railroad**, board a raft across to **Tom Sawyer Island**. Most popular of the rides here is **Splash Mountain**. Your boat will seem to hang interminably in space before dropping five stories into a pool.

Liberty Square. A few steps away, the architecture changes from Old West to New England. The **Hall of Presidents** is a major attraction, with America's leaders brought to life through animatronics. The Liberty Square Riverboat's leisurely trip can make a welcome break from long lines. The **Haunted Mansion** near by is more funny than frightening, even when one of its ghosts sits next to you.

Fantasyland. The Magic Kingdom is fantasy throughout, but here it reaches its purest form. Among the most winning attractions here is **Mickey's PhilharMagic**, a 3-D animation, music, and special-effects show. The **Mad Tea Party** is a dizzying whirl in a gigantic teacup, while '**It's a Small World**' sets everyone smiling as they cruise past singing, dancing dolls.

Frontierland's Big Thunder Mountain Railroad

Small children adore **Peter Pan's Flight**, **Dumbo the Flying Elephant**, and **Cinderella's Golden Carousel**, a classic merry-go-round. The **Many Adventures of Winnie the Pooh** is a whimsical ride through the pages of a giant storybook, while the mood is decidedly darker at **Snow White's Scary Adventures**. The last attraction is perhaps the simplest and sweetest: **Storytime with Belle** in the **Fairytale Garden**. From Fantasyland, you can take the **Skyway** cable car to Tomorrowland or walk through Cinderella's Castle past scenes from the film.

Mickey's Toontown Fair. This land is tucked away, so you could easily miss it. Mickey's House is set up like a museum of memorabilia, but it is at **Toontown County Fair** where you'll meet the Mouse himself, ready to sign autographs and pose for pictures. Youngsters love **The Barnstormer**, a zippy coaster that's just their size.

Tomorrowland. This land is dominated by a white cone of steel, the famous **Space Mountain**. Inside, a thrilling roller-coaster ride races through inky blackness. Heed the warning signs, and don't attempt the ride if you've got a weak neck, back, heart, or stomach. **Stitch's Great Escape!** invites guests into the middle of some comic chaos as a wacky space alien bursts loose. **Monsters, Inc. Laugh Floor**, an alien comedy club in the city of Monstropolis, is another popular attraction. **Buzz Lightyear's Space Ranger Spin** is an interactive journey through the world of Disney's *Toy Story*. Riders join Buzz in his outer-space mission to save the universe, firing twin laser cannons at passing targets. **Tomorrowland Indy Speedway** – gas-powered cars that plod along a track – is a favorite for kids.

Before leaving the Magic Kingdom, take a 20-minute trip round its borders on the **Walt Disney World Railroad**. The steam engines that haul the open passenger cars are the real thing and were built around the turn of the 20th century.

Epcot

Twenty years in the planning and opened in 1982, Walt Disney World's 'Experimental Prototype Community of Tomorrow' is a park full of attractions to enlighten and entertain. The park has two distinct theme areas, together forming a figure 8. In the first, **Future World**, the pavilions are sponsored by some of America's biggest corporations such as General Motors, ExxonMobil, and Kodak. The second, **World Showcase**, celebrates the cultures and products of eleven different nations. Epcot is reached by car and shuttle bus and from the Magic Kingdom by monorail.

Future World's **Spaceship Earth** is the park's icon. The huge aluminum-clad orb is an architectural summation of Disney's visionary aspirations. Inside is a pedestrian ride detailing the history of communications, sponsored by Siemens.

The **Seas with Nemo and Friends** pavilion, a recent arrival, features a same-name show that lets you meet some of your Disney-Pixar marine friends on a journey under the sea, where you will also encounter several species of sea life, including sharks, dolphins, and barracuda. At the end of the voyage, youngsters and young-at-heart adults can interact with one of the stars at **Turtle Talk with Crush**.

Outside are a range of interactive exhibits, but most people in this area will be building up courage to take a ride on **Mission: SPACE**. NASA consultants were brought in to help design the simulated mission to Mars, where you experience the g-force of lift-off as an astronaut would. This experience is realistic enough that Disney hands out airplane barf bags. If that seems beyond your limits, Epcot has added a calmer version of the ride.

Continuing around the outer edge of Future World brings you to General Motors' **Test Track**, a simulation of an automotive proving ground and one of the park's most popular attractions. Six people ride a test car through a high-speed hill climb and over banked curves, hitting speeds of up to 65mph (105km/h). The line is always one of the longest in the park.

Between here and Spaceship Earth lie the twin buildings of **Innoventions**, where you can see high-tech solutions to everyday problems. Flanking Innoventions to the west are two other pavilions: The Land and Imagination!

The Land pavilion focuses on agriculture, nutrition, and the environment. In **Living With the Land** you cruise by boat past a series of ecosystems, then into an experimental greenhouse. If you are especially interested, sign up for a 45-minute walking tour. Environmental stewardship is the message of **The Circle of Life**, a 20-minute film featuring characters from *The Lion King*. One of the park's newest attractions, **Soarin'**, is a simulated hang-glider ride

Epcot's Spaceship Earth

over redwood forests, the Pacific surf, and San Francisco's Golden Gate Bridge.

Imagination! is a light-hearted ride that challenges guests to increase their 'I.Q.' (Imagination Quotient). In the same pavilion is **Honey, I Shrunk the Kids**, a wild 3-D adventure that convincingly simulates the microscopic experience.

World Showcase

Ranged round the perimeter of a lagoon stand replicas of some of the world's great monuments. A scale model of the Eiffel Tower rises above the Florida landscape; a diminutive version of Venice's Campanile stands near a Mayan pyramid from Mexico, and so on. Eleven nations are represented, all with restaurants featuring national cuisine, film presentations, entertainers, and/or shops.

IllumiNations

Each evening, Epcot stages IllumiNations: Reflections of Earth, around the World Showcase Lagoon. The night sky is filled with fireworks, lasers, and choreographed 'dancing' fountains.

Norway offers a boat trip on the stormy *Maelstrom*. The Akershus Restaurant puts on a typical Norwegian buffet.

Mexico's pyramid houses priceless pre-Columbian treasures and a riverboat trip through Mexican history, with an authentic Mexican eatery.

China's circular Temple of Heaven is just right for the film *Wonders of China*. The restaurant offers meals prepared in provincial Chinese cooking styles.

Germany's village concentrates on traditional food and beer, and shops selling fine glass, silver, porcelain, chocolates, and wine.

Italy also emphasizes eating and drinking, in a branch of L'Originale Alfredo di Roma. Street performers entertain the crowds in 'St Mark's Square.'

The American Adventure takes center stage. *The American Adventure Show* takes a half-hour journey through American history in film and special effects, including some of the most lifelike animatronics figures yet made by Disney.

Japan shows a formal face, with tranquil gardens and temples. Three eating places serve Japanese dishes, and there's a branch of a famous Tokyo department store.

Morocco's authentic buildings are a World Showcase highlight. They house a colorful bazaar and the Restaurant Marrakesh, where a belly dancer diverts the diners.

France concentrates on gastronomy in three French restaurants, each with an all-French staff.

The United Kingdom cultivates an 'olde worlde' image with Tudor buildings and the Rose and Crown Pub.

Canada shows a Circle-Vision 360 film. Inuit (Eskimo) and Indian crafts are featured in the shops. The restaurant offers a full menu of Canadian foods.

Disney's Hollywood Studios

Celebrating the American love affair with show business, this theme park opened in 1989. They occasionally make films and TV programs here, but above all it's fun.

Inside the entrance, leave the shops until later and walk down **Hollywood Boulevard** towards the big open space of Sunset Plaza. On the right you'll see a giant board with all the

Hollywood Boulevard

latest information on shows and waiting times. Towering over a circular plaza at the end of the boulevard is a 12-story **Sorcerer's Hat** like the one worn by Mickey Mouse in *Fantasia*.

Sunset Boulevard veers off to the right of the plaza. At the end of the boulevard is the **Rock'n'Roller Coaster Starring Aerosmith**. This is an indoor roller-coaster that features a high-speed launch of 0–60 mph (0–97 km/h) in 2.8 seconds and three inversions – all to a synchronized Aerosmith tune. It's not for lightweights. Another attraction that is always packed is **The Twilight Zone Tower of Terror**. This is for those who enjoy 13-story drops through pitch darkness.

On the other side of Echo Lake is **Star Tours**, a simulator thrill created by George Lucas in the tradition of *Star Wars*, which takes place on an imaginary but all-too-convincing trip to Endor, where you're thrown around while a synchronized film shows the frightening view from the out-of-control spacecraft. In a 2,000-seat theater the **Indiana Jones Epic Stunt Spectacular** re-enacts several scenes from *Raiders of the Lost Ark*. Similarly, the new **Lights, Motors, Action! Extreme Stunt Show** uses actors, pyrotechnics, and fast cars in an edge-of-your-seat production.

Journey into Narnia: Prince Caspian offers a behind-the-scenes, multi-screen peek at that film, while **Toy Story Mania** is a tame, 3-D ride that stars several characters, including Mr Potato Head. And, **Catastrophe Canyon** in the Backlot Tour is where 'by mistake' you get mixed up in a disaster movie complete with earthquake, explosions, and a flash flood.

In **The Great Movie Ride**, near the Sorcerer's Hat, your seats carry you through animated scenes from dozens of classic movies. The ride takes place inside a reproduction of the famous Mann's Chinese Theater. The 22-minute ride explores the history of cinema, with a cast of both live and animated characters recreating memorable movie scenes inside (and outside the theater while you're queued up). There are two different storylines for this tour – either cowboys or gangsters. Some portions are three-dimensional, so be prepared to be surprised.

Before 5pm or so, when the artists pack up work for the day, go to **The Magic of Disney Animation** for a walking tour with an insight into the process by which animated films are made. After dark, **Fantasmic**, Disney-MGM's big finale, takes place in a 6,900-seat amphitheater, a spectacle with fireworks, lasers, and fire.

A vulture at Disney's Animal Kingdom

Disney's Animal Kingdom
The fourth and newest theme park is **Disney's Animal Kingdom**, where live animals, prehistoric creatures, and the classic Disney characters are featured in a lush and beautiful setting. The park is laid out in a classic

'hub-and-spoke' style, and visitors enter **The Oasis Exhibits**, populated with deer, anteaters, tree kangaroos, and other animals. The park's four 'lands' radiate from **Discovery Island**, where the **Tree of Life** towers 145ft (44m) above guests and houses the 3-D film **It's Tough to Be a Bug**. From Safari Village, visitors head clockwise to **Camp Minnie-Mickey**, featuring the popular **Festival of the Lion King** stage show, an uplifting 30-minute pageant based loosely on the film.

Next is **Africa**, home of **Kilimanjaro Safaris**, a fascinating 20-minute trip across the African savannah, where black rhinos, hippos, elephants, and lions roam. At the end of the safari you can follow **Pangani Forest Exploration Trail**, home to such endangered species as dik-diks and black-and-white colobus monkeys, as well as hippos and a family of lowland gorillas. Guides are on hand to answer questions.

Asia is the newest land, featuring **Kali River Rapids**, a white-water rafting adventure, and the park's newest thrill ride, **Expedition Everest**. It's a forward–backward roller-coaster that's not for the weak of stomach.

Completing the circle around Discovery Island is **DinoLand U.S.A.**, with **The Boneyard**, where you can play among the fossil remains of Triceratops, T-Rex, and other vanished giants. **Primeval Whirl** spins you through a maze of curves, hills, and drops – and **DINOSAUR** takes you on a rough ride back in time to rescue a specimen before it is made extinct.

Downtown Disney

Conscious that it was losing guests in the evenings to the attractions of downtown Orlando and elsewhere, the Disney organization decided to create some nightlife of its own. **Downtown Disney** is the result, a metropolis of restaurants, nightclubs, theaters, and shops that includes **Marketplace**, **Pleasure Island**, and **West Side**. **Marketplace** has more than 25 shops and restaurants, including the largest Disney merchandise shop in the world. Adjacent is **Pleasure Island**, with shopping, dining, themed nightclubs, and live bands on an open-air stage. The setting is the abandoned, ramshackle old warehouses of some run-down port, all specially built in 1989. There's an entrance charge in the evening, but it's free during the day. Next door is **West Side**, with restaurants, shops, a 24-screen cinema, and the giant **DisneyQuest** building filled with high-tech, interactive attractions. One of the star attractions on the West Side is the the permanent **Cirque du Soleil**, a blend of traditional circus art with theater, mime, and cabaret.

More Attractions at Walt Disney World

Typhoon Lagoon is a giant aqua park with beaches, water-slides, and streams where you can drift along sitting in a rubber tube. Its claim to fame, though, is a huge lagoon where

The House of Blues in Downtown Disney

a huge wave-making machine generates rollers up to 6ft (1.8m) high for body-surfing. **Blizzard Beach** is based on an abandoned ski resort and features the tallest freefall water slide in the world. **Disney's Wide World of Sports** often has a sports event, and visitors are invited to watch: the Atlanta Braves hold spring training here, for instance, and it's the home of the US Men's Clay Court Championships and a training site for the Harlem Globetrotters.

Universal Orlando

In 1999, Universal Studios (daily 9am–6pm, sometimes later; charge; www.universalorlando.com) more than doubled its original size, growing from a single theme park to a mega-resort with two theme parks, a huge entertainment district and a hotel (now there are three hotels to choose from), changing its name in the process to **Universal Orlando**.

The Incredible Hulk coaster

Islands of Adventure

The newest 110-acre (44-hectare) park is **Islands of Adventure**, featuring five islands in a lagoon – **Seuss Landing**, **Lost Continent**, **Jurassic Park**, **Toon Lagoon**, and **Marvel Super Hero Island**. (A new **Harry Potter** area opens in 2009/2010.) Many rides are among the most technologically advanced ever made.

Universal appeal

When Universal Studios opened in 1990, comparisons were inevitably made with Disney's Hollywood Studios. Universal tends to be less whimsical, appealing more to teenagers and film buffs than to small children. Though it has added more kid-friendly attractions, overall this park makes entertaining adults its priority.

From the Port of Entry, heading clockwise is Marvel Super Hero Island, with two of the park's hottest attractions: the **Incredible Hulk Coaster** that shoots riders up a 150ft (46m) tunnel at g-forces approaching those of an F-16 fighter jet, then spins them upside down in a weightless roll more than 10 stories above ground; and **The Amazing Adventures of Spider-Man**, with astonishing 3-D effects in a high-speed ride that is arguably one of the best special-effects productions in Orlando. **Toon Lagoon** is next, with **Popeye & Bluto's Bilge-Rat Barges** (be prepared to get soaked in this raft ride) and **Dudley Do-Right's Ripsaw Falls**, a flume ride that sends riders plummeting below the water surface. All this cold water feels great in the summertime, but a little less so on a wintry day. **Jurassic Park** features plenty of dinosaurs, and the **Jurassic Park River Adventure**, with the longest, fastest plunge – 85ft (26m) – ever built in a theme-park ride. This area is also home to **Pteranodon Flyers**, a rickety gondola ride that offers a bird's-eye view of the island.

The **Lost Continent** is themed with dragons and mythical gods. One of the park's star attractions, **Dueling Drag-**

ons, is the world's first dual-racing coaster, with tracks that intertwine so that riders are less than a foot apart at two points while traveling at speeds close to 60mph (97km/h).

Tamer adventures are in **Seuss Landing**, including the **Cat in the Hat** that moves riders, seated on couches, past scenes from the book; **One Fish, Two Fish, Red Fish, Blue Fish** kiddie ride and the **High in the Sky Seuss Trolley Train**.

Universal Studios Florida
Next door to Islands of Adventure, the original park consists of over 400 acres (160 hectares) of realistic sets and real production equipment – the biggest facility of its kind east of California.

Revenge of the Mummy

Because the area here is bigger than at Disney, the streets may be less crowded, and at times it can seem there is less going on, but Universal Studios can claim some of the most thrilling adventures anywhere. One of the best is **Terminator 2: 3-D Battle Across Time**, where you'll find yourself alongside Arnold Schwarzenegger, dodging laser fire in a cyber battle. Ogre fans get their due inside **Shrek 4-D**, a multi-sensory ride that allows you and your fellow adventurers to follow the G-rated honeymoon adventures of Shrek and Princess Fiona.

The park's newest addition, **The Simpsons Ride**, loops, dips, and swirls through a world that this animated family's fans surely will enjoy. **Men in Black Alien Attack** lets you blast bug-eyed space creatures with laser cannons, then scores your marksmanship at the end.

Other top attractions include Universal's **Revenge of the Mummy**, set in the New York working backlot. This indoor ride takes full advantage of set design, high-speed coaster tricks and optical illusions to terrify its riders. Also in New York, on 57th Street is **Twister... Ride It Out**, based on the 1996 action movie where the amazing fury of an F-5 tornado is recreated.

Universal Studios CityWalk

The 30-acre (12-hectare) CityWalk entertainment district sits between Islands of Adventure and Universal Studios. It rivals Downtown Disney, with an eclectic collection of restaurants, shops, nightclubs, and cinemas. The latest arrivals are the **Red Coconut Club**, a dance club with signature martinis, and the three-strong **Blue Man Group**, instantly recognised for being painted blue and dressed in black, and known for their avant-garde stage shows and concerts that combine music, comedy, and multimedia theatrics. CityWalk also has the world's largest **Hard Rock Café** (decorated with an incredible collection of rock memorabilia) and the **Hard Rock Live Orlando** concert hall. Soft-rock balladeer **Jimmy Buffet's Margaritaville**, with restaurant and three bars, is the place to party, while nearby **Emeril's Orlando** is fine dining influenced by New Orleans Creole cooking. There is also a 20-screen **Universal Cineplex** theater showing the latest films.

You can purchase a Party Pass that allows access to all of the clubs, including **CityWalk's Rising Star**, **Pat O'Brien's**, **the groove** and **Bob Marley – A Tribute to Freedom**.

Encounter at SeaWorld

SeaWorld Orlando

Close to International Drive, its main entrance on Central Florida Parkway, **SeaWorld Orlando** (daily 9am–6pm, sometimes later; charge; www. seaworldorlando.com) is the leader in Florida's marine parks. Highlights include performing dolphins and sea lions; polar bears cavorting in an icy Arctic playground; and 'Believe' extrasensory show starring killer whale Shamu and trainers. **Journey to Atlantis** is a water-coaster thrill ride with one of the wettest, fastest drops in the world – a six-story dive that creates a tidal wave.

Kraken is the fastest, tallest, longest coaster in Orlando. SeaWorld has two sister parks. **Discovery Cove** (daily 9am–6pm; charge; www.discoverycove.com) lets visitors swim with dolphins, snorkel with tropical fish, and hand feed exotic birds. New arrival **Aquatica** (daily 9am–6pm, sometimes later; charge; www.aquaticabyseaworld.com) offers two wave machines, a river-rapids run, and an enclosed flume ride through a Commerson's dolphin exhibit.

Wet 'n' Wild

This collection of lakes and pools, off International Drive, features water slides, rapids, a wave machine, and other sports facilities (daily 9 or 10am–6pm, sometimes later; charge; www.wetnwildolando.com). Daredevils recommend the **Fuji Flyer**, which sends four passengers plunging down six stories, or the **Black Hole**, which propels riders through 600ft (182m) of twisting, turning, watery darkness. Families might prefer the **Bubba Tub**, a tame raft ride.

SOUTHWEST FLORIDA

The Everglades

Called 'the river of grass' by the Indians, this watery plain is the most famous swamp in the world. Not quite flat, its waters flow almost imperceptibly from Lake Okeechobee south and west into Florida Bay.

The 1,400,000-acre (560,000-hectare) **Everglades National Park** (daily 8.30am–6pm; charge; www.nps.gov/ever) is a protected area of marshy land and broken coastline. Winter, the dry season, is the best time to visit. You'll see the most birdlife then, and there are fewer mosquitoes.

You can reach the Everglades from both the Miami area and the West Coast. The **Everglades City** entrance is best if you're planning to explore the park by boat. If a day trip is your only visit, **Shark Valley** has a two-hour, motorized tram

Exploring the Everglades on an airboat safari

tour that gives an excellent overview of the Everglades. **Royal Palm Visitor Center** is closer if you're on the East Coast, with two easy walks: the Anhinga Trail boardwalk, which circles over the sawgrass marsh, and the Gumbo Limbo Trail, a circular half-mile track. Look out for raccoons, opossums, tree-snails, and lizards.

If you drive beyond Royal Palm, you'll pass more trails and sightseeing points, all marked on the park map, before you reach **Flamingo**, a fishing village on a shallow bay, with a colorful history of illicit liquor ('moonshine') production. Now life revolves around a ranger station, a lodge, a restaurant, and a grocery store. At Flamingo Marina you can buy bait and rent tackle, boats, and canoes. Take plenty of insect repellent. Hunting and firearms are banned.

At the **Miccosukee Indian Village** near Shark Valley you can see craft demonstrations and alligator wrestling. The Miccosukee have lived in isolation here since the time of the

Everglades Environment

Marjorie Stoneham Douglas gave this wilderness area an enduring name when she wrote the now classic book, *The Everglades: River of Grass*. This area is a constantly changing marsh with uplands, a natural part of Florida that has become increasingly fragile due to pollution from development and, some argue, the South Florida sugar industry. Clean-up, or the lack of it, remains an ongoing political battle, but it still remains a haven for critically endangered species such as the American crocodile, West Indian manatee, and Florida panther, as well as wading birds, mammals, and reptiles. Palaeo-Indians lived here as early as 10,000BC, when mammoths and ancient bison were their neighbors. It also was a home for Seminole Indians during their early 19th-century battles with US troops. The park was dedicated in 1947 by President Harry S. Truman after Douglas's book was published.

Seminole War, but fewer than 100 were left when the US government recognized the tribe in 1962. Now there are over 500. The Tamiami Trail heads west along the southern perimeter of the Big Cypress National Preserve.

The Gulf Coast

The central Gulf Coast has long been a favorite vacation spot for northerners and Europeans, while southern areas were a well-kept secret until fairly recently. The rapidly developing towns gleam in the sun, and business parks, shopping centers, and residential developments are spreading inland. Old fishing

Naples fishing pier

towns are being gradually eclipsed by new construction.

Much of the coastline is protected by long offshore sandbars, which means crossing salt lagoons, by causeway or boat, to find the beach. From **Marco Island** near the Everglades up to Tampa Bay, 180 miles (290km) of inlets, lakes, peninsulas, and islands make for a sailing and fishing paradise. The warm, calm waters and gently sloping white sands on Gulf Coast Islands are perfect for children, and there are plenty of diversions away from the beaches.

The elegant town of **Naples** has a fishing pier and a famous shell beach, with collectors out early in the morning to see what the tide has left behind. Golfers come out early as well to play on one of the town's 50-odd golf courses. The Village on Venetian Bay shows how attractive a shopping mall can be, and for a view of the most luxurious waterfront homes, take a dinner cruise on a sternwheeler around the maze of inlets.

The **Collier County Museum** (Mon–Fri 9am–5pm, Sat 9am–4pm; free), located off the Tamiami Trail at the Collier County Government Center, has 5 acres (2 hectares) devoted to local history, including a large garden of native Florida flora, a Seminole Village, and an archaeological laboratory. At the junction of Fleischmann Boulevard and US 41, **Naples Zoo at Caribbean Gardens** (daily 9.30am–5.30pm; charge; www.napleszoo.com) features big-game animals and wild birds in a tropical garden.

If you'd prefer to see creatures in the wild, follow State Road 846 to **Corkscrew Swamp Sanctuary** (daily 7am–5.30pm, later in summer; charge). The National Audubon Society has preserved 11,000 acres (4,400 hectares) of wilderness here, al-

The boardwalks at Corkscrew Swamp allow safe exploration

lowing amateur ornithologists to delight in the estimated 200 bird species that reside here. Almost 2 miles (3km) of boardwalks pass through the great bald cypress trees.

Fort Myers

Fort Myers still has a feeling of old Florida about it. Its **Historical Museum** documents its past, but kids will probably better enjoy the **Imaginarium Hands-On Museum and Aquarium**, with its numerous interactive exhibitions. Just south of downtown **Fort Myers** you can visit the **Edison** and **Ford Winter Estates** (daily 9am–5.30pm; charge; www.efwefla.org). The inventive genius who gave the world the light bulb, the phonograph, the stock ticker, and much more, Thomas Alva Edison (1847–1931) moved here for his health in 1886. He built a laboratory and developed the garden of exotic plants and trees in his search for new materials. The huge Banyan tree was just a seedling when Harvey Firestone, founder of the tire company, gave it to Edison. The tour takes in Edison's laboratory, a collection of old cars and phonographs, and his study filled with personal effects. The great inventor's friend Henry Ford built a house right next door – you can visit that too, though it's not as compelling.

In the same area, **Babcock Wilderness Adventures** (off State Road 31; hours vary; charge; www.babcockwilderness. com) takes you on a ride through swamp and forest, with stops to look at the wildlife, including panthers, wild turkeys, and snakes. Alligators lying on the trails will make you appreciate the conditions the early pioneers had to contend with. You need to phone for reservations, tel: (800) 500-5583 (toll-free in the US).

Offshore Retreats

Only specks on the Florida map, the string of islands that stretch like a fish-hook from the mouth of the Caloosahatchee

Historic building, Boca Grande

River across Charlotte Harbor are beloved and fiercely protected by their residents. **Sanibel**, the southernmost, is famous for its seashells, and for the J.N. Darling National Wildlife Refuge. It's also well known for its traffic jams in high season, although you can't see much from a car and there are few places to stop. To appreciate this area and its wildlife, you really need to take to the water. Tiny **Captiva Island** is linked to Sanibel by a causeway, but so far **North Captiva** and **Cayo Costa** can only be reached by boat. **Boca Grande** (accessible by toll bridge via Englewood) has long been a winter hideaway for rich northerners.

North on the mainland, **Venice** has some fine public beaches, and it's a great place to search for fossilized shark teeth. You can cast a line at the Venice fishing pier, or visit Grinder, the resident dolphin, in the Venice jetties.

CENTRAL WEST FLORIDA

Sarasota

This self-styled cultural capital of Florida is a favorite with visitors. The locals insist **Sarasota** is queen of the coast, with its own orchestra and winter seasons of ballet, opera, and theater.

Near the center, the **Van Wezel Performing Arts Hall** (performance times and dates vary; charge; www.vanwezel.org) is a landmark. Completed in 1970 and dubbed the 'purple people-seater,' it rises by the bay like a dramatic lavender shell.

Sarasota's **Jungle Gardens** (daily 9am–5pm; charge; www.sarasotajunglegardens.com) is another of Florida's beautiful botanical gardens, stocked with a few jungle animals, and the **Marie Selby Botanical Gardens** (daily 10am–5pm; charge; www.selby.org) on the bay front have thousands of orchids and water lilies shaded by Banyan trees and bamboo.

Across Ringling Causeway off US 41, Sarasota's prettiest shopping and restaurant center, **St Armand's Circle**, is on the way to Lido Key and beach. The next barrier island to the south, **Siesta Key**, claims the whitest sand in the world. It's superb for castle-building and low tide brings shell-seekers.

John and Mable Ringling of circus fame established their **estate** just north of Sarasota in the early 1920s. Within just a few years the couple had built a Venetian-style palazzo and a museum filled with hundreds of works of art that reflected their passion for the Italian Renaissance and Baroque.

The **Ringling Museum of Art** (daily 10am–5.30pm; charge; www.ringling.org) has several of the Rubens cartoons for the *Triumph of the Eucharist* cycle (the other two extant are in the Louvre in Paris). Hals, Cranach, and Veronese are also represented in this superbly arranged collection of 14th- to 19th-century paintings. Don't miss the less publicized paintings by

Ringling Museum of Art

Asolo Theatre

The Asolo Theatre www.asolo.org, near the Ringling Museum of Art, is a Rococo gem brought stone by stone from Asolo, northwest of Venice, Italy, and reassembled here in the early 1950s.

Joseph Wright of Derby, Rosa Bonheur, and Sir Edward Burne-Jones (the extraordinary *The Sirens*).

Ca' d'Zan ('John's House' in Venetian patois) has been called grandiose, but if the Ringlings wanted a house in Venetian palace style, why not? It's undeniably impressive on the shores of the bay, and provides an insight into the tastes and indulgences of America's rich during the 1920s.

The Circus Museum, with its gilt circus wagons and old posters, was an afterthought on the part of the state of Florida, to which Ringling left his estate and collections. A huge range of old cars and 2,000 mechanical musical instruments – player pianos, organs, musical boxes, and phonographs – can be seen at **Sarasota Classic Car Museum** (daily 9am–6pm; charge; www.sarasotacarmuseum.org), just across US 41. East of Sarasota on Route 72, you can bike, drive, or take a boat trip through the **Myakka River State Park** (daily 8am–5pm; charge), or hike along its 37 miles (60km) of nature trails.

St Petersburg

Farther up the coast, the impressive **Sunshine Skyway** toll bridge soars high over the mouth of Tampa Bay. On the north side, St Petersburg is a bustling, sprawling city. The strange-looking inverted pyramid apparently floating in the water is **The Pier**, a complex of shops with restaurants on top. The pier is the starting point for fishing trips and pleasure cruises.

A few blocks away on 4th Street, **Sunken Gardens** (Mon–Sat 10am–4.30pm, Sun noon–4.30pm; charge; www.stpete.org/sunken) is a tropical riot of color and scents, an oasis of natural life surrounded by trendy shops and cafés. The **Salvador**

The Sunshine Skyway bridge

Dalí Museum (1000 3rd Street South; Mon–Sat 9.30am–5.30pm, sometimes later, Sun noon–5.30pm; charge; www.salvadordalimuseum.org) was donated to the city by two friends of Dalí from Cleveland, Ohio. Opened in 1982, this huge accumulation of works by the Spanish Surrealist includes paintings, sculptures, books, and graphics. On the street leading to the pier is the **Museum of Fine Arts** (Tue–Sat 10am–5pm, Sun 1–5pm; charge; www.fine-arts.org), with a delightful collection of works by Renoir and Cézanne, and American painters Georgia O'Keeffe, Whistler, and Grandma Moses.

Pinellas Suncoast

St Petersburg faces the bay, but several miles away on the Gulf Coast, **St Pete Beach** is the start of a 20-mile (32km) string of barrier islands stretching north to **Clearwater Beach**, and sometimes known collectively as the Pinellas Suncoast. Reached by four causeways, the strip is built up from end to

Sponge diver at Tarpon Springs

end but the gently sloping, sandy beach is superb, up to 200yds (180m) wide, with occasional piers for fishing. At John's Pass, the sea separates Madeira and Treasure Island, and a bridge links them. The Village and Boardwalk here are a complex of restaurants, bars, and shops.

Caladesi Island State Park near Dunedin (daily 8am–5pm; charge) is a secluded barrier island that is a great place to look for seashells, observe seabirds, and enjoy a landscape filled with mangroves and dunes.

North of Clearwater, **Tarpon Springs** became the home of the sponge industry when Greek divers came here at the beginning of the 20th century. At **Spongeorama** you can learn about the history of sponge-diving and visit exhibits about the marine creature whose skeleton ends up in your bath. The old Sponge Exchange is now a shopping and dining district.

Thirty miles (48km) up the coast, **Weeki Wachee** (hours vary; charge) is an attraction with a water park and local fauna, but the main exhibit is an underwater show by swimmers dressed as mermaids. Despite its charm, this 'City of Mermaids' has struggled in recent years to stay open.

Tampa

The big city of the Gulf Coast is still quite compact, but growing fast, upwards in the center and outwards away from the bay. Historic **Ybor City**, a quaint suburb of Tampa where there were once 200 cigar factories employing thousands of Cuban workers, has been renovated to a vibrant area of shops, restaurants, and nightclubs. On Tampa's waterfront, one of the newer attractions is the glass-domed **Florida Aquarium** (daily 9.30am–5pm; charge; www.fl aquarium.org), with thousands of underwater creatures representing 550 species native to Florida, including a view of the ocean from 60ft (20m) under the sea.

Busch Gardens

In a huge park northeast of Tampa, brewing giant Anheuser-Busch has piled on the attractions in an effort to outdo its Orlando rivals. **Busch Gardens** (daily 9am–6pm, sometimes later; charge; www.busch gardens.com) has the best collection of roller-coasters in all Florida, six of them altogether, grouped around a unifying theme of the African continent, with the buildings resembling those of southern Morocco.

Kumba at Busch Gardens

Montu is the Southeast's longest and tallest inverted roller-coaster, which can reach speeds of up to 60mph (97km/h). **Kumba** is a giant steel roller-coaster with a 135ft (41m) drop. **SheiKra** riders are strapped into floorless 24-seat cars for a three-minute ride that starts from 200ft (60m) – making it the tallest roller coaster in Florida – then sends them down at a 90-degree angle. **Gwazi** is a classic wooden roller-coaster named for a mythical lion with a tiger's head. All this makes **Cheetah Chase**'s kiddie loops and **Scorpion**'s old-fashioned loop seem tame.

You can go white-water rafting on the **Congo River Rapids** or scream down a water flume ride with a 40ft (12m) drop. Or get soaked on the **Tanganyika Tidal Wave**, with a 55ft (19m) dive that creates a massive wave of water, soaking both riders and spectators. For tamer visitors, the open plains of the **Serengeti**, with their big game animals and herds of grazing zebras and antelopes, can be viewed from Sky Ride, an old-fashioned train, or **The Rhino Rally** ride. Try all three, or reserve a spot on the Serengeti Safari truck ride for a chance to hand-feed the animals. **Edge of Africa** puts you in the heart of the veld, where you'll see lions, hyenas, crocodiles, hippos, giraffes, and more. The barriers between you and the animals are natural and mostly hidden.

You are invited to tour the on-site brewery and to sample the beers at Hospitality House if you are 21 years of age or over. You can easily take a full day to see Busch Gardens and get value for your money.

Nearby **Adventure Island** (hours vary, closed winter; charge; www.4adventure.com) has waterfalls, water slides, and waves.

NORTHWEST FLORIDA

Slip off your shoes and step onto pure white sand that squeaks under your feet as you explore the Panhandle and its beautiful seashores. Beaches such as the **Gulf Islands National Seashore** (daily 8am–5pm; charge), **Grayton Beach State Recreation Area** (daily 8am–5pm; charge), **Cape San Blas**, and **St Andrews State Park** (daily 8am–5pm; charge) are vivid reminders of how much of Florida's coast looked in the 1940s and 1950s.

The pace here is slower than in other parts of the state. There are no big cities, although **Destin** and **Fort Walton Beach** are growing and have long had great appeal to vacationers from Alabama and Georgia, while Panama City is something of a spring-break magnet for college kids. But it's more common to find charming, if in some cases manufactured, towns and resorts such as **Seaside** and **Rosemary Beach**.

The Panhandle does have the requisite tourist attractions to distract visitors from the beaches. The best of these include the **National Museum of Naval Aviation** (daily 9am–5pm; free) in **Pensacola** and **Gulf World Marine Park** in **Panama City** (days and hours vary; charge), where dolphins, penguins, and sea lions are the stars of the shows.

For some of the best seafood, the town of **Apalachicola** has scrumptious oysters, shrimp and fish, not to mention the visual appeal of a small fishing village.

Deserted beach at Pensacola

WHAT TO DO

SPORTS

With a winter like other people's summers and seas as tempting as a tropical lagoon, Florida will have you out and playing before you can get your bags unpacked.

Golf and tennis practically have the status of religions here, and the waters are ideal for sailing, canoeing, and fishing. You can go hiking, riding, and hunting (here it means shooting). Spectator sports at various times of year include football, baseball, basketball, and even polo. You can watch and bet on greyhounds and horses and the Basque specialty, *jai alai*, a super-fast version of squash played with a hybrid of a hockey stick and sling, and a ball called a *pelota*.

Sports cars race the famous tracks at Daytona and Sebring. Then there's the most popular outdoor activity of all – hitting the beach and cooling off in the sea.

Watersports

Whether you prefer windsurfing, snorkeling, scuba diving, water-skiing, or just plain swimming, Florida's beaches, springs, rivers, and lakes have enough room for everybody.

Chances for **scuba diving** exist along the Atlantic Coast, but the best area is around the Florida Keys, including more than 20 miles (32km) of coral reef in John Pennekamp Coral Reef State Park *(see page 34)*. You'll need a certified diver's card or you can take classes when you arrive – details can be obtained from any diving shop.

Snorkeling amid the brilliant fish is exhilarating, too. Touching the fragile coral is forbidden, and it's illegal to take any of it. You can rent all the equipment you'll need, but shop around for the best prices.

Big waves for **surfing** are mainly restricted to the Atlantic Coast – Cocoa Beach and Melbourne Beach are favorites, though they are nothing like Hawaii or Australia. Calmer waters protected by barrier islands or the beaches along the Gulf Coast are ideal for **water-skiing** or **windsurfing**.

With a coastline that's longer than any state's save Alaska, **beaches** are countless – and often seemingly endless (Daytona Beach runs for 23 miles/37km), though access may be restricted in places by private property. If the crowd of sun-worshippers is too dense for you in one spot, a short walk will earn you some space – most people don't stray far from their cars.

Popular beaches usually have lifeguards, especially at weekends. Some have barbecue facilities, too, but alcohol, glass containers, and pets are frequently banned.

Beware of the power of the sun, especially if you are snorkeling: Your back can feel cool and still burn quite badly, unless you've applied waterproof sunblock.

Don't Touch

A coral reef is alive and growing, the creation of billions of tiny polyps. Related to jellyfish and sea anemones, these little animals live in cup-shaped shells of limestone that they build for themselves. Coral's gorgeous colors come from algae living within the coral tissue. Each new generation builds on the skeletons of the last, but the outer living layer is thin and very fragile. A boat's anchor can leave a dead white scar. Even the touch of a diver's hand or foot can spread decay. In shallower water, corals resemble boulders and delicate fans. Farther out, where they have to stand up to a battering from waves, come the branching elkhorn varieties. Even from a glass-bottom boat you'll see hosts of fish enjoying the reef's protection. Their bright colors probably relate to the need to distinguish foes from possible mates in the crowd.

Boating and Sailing. No holiday in Florida would be complete without at least one outing on the water. Powerboats, sailboats, and canoes are available for hire. You can sail nearly everywhere. Some of the best powerboating is from Everglades City among the Ten Thousand Islands and down south in Florida Bay. Navigational charts can be purchased at marinas and map dealers.

Airboat rides are a noisy but exciting way of skimming shallows and swamps, and **glass-bottom boats** let you see the coral reefs without getting wet.

Kayaking in the Everglades

There are also some 35 officially designated **kayaking** trails through the Everglades and on the rivers flowing from Central Florida's springs and lakes. The state's Department of Environmental Protection publishes a free guide to the trails (3900 Commonwealth Boulevard, Tallahassee, FL 32399-3000; www.dep.state.fl.us). To hire canoes, look in the *Yellow Pages* under Boat Dealers, or ask at the local chamber of commerce.

Fishing. Hundreds of different species of fish inhabit the rivers, creeks, and seas (see www.floridafishing.com). You can hire rods and reels, or, if you're an enthusiast, this is a good place to buy equipment. Bait shops at the docks and fishing piers will give you free advice on what to fish for.

Fishing charters at Key West

Often your biggest problem will be competition from pelicans, which hang about in the hopes of stealing away with some of your catch. In the process they may get hooked themselves: if it happens, release them with extreme care.

Marinas everywhere are crowded with expensive deep-sea fishing boats for hire – they come complete with a knowledgeable captain. Beyond that the only thing you'll need is plenty of patience. Some boats go for the more certain mackerel and amberjack, but you can try for the big ones – marlin and shark, or the exciting if inedible tarpon, which can weigh from 60 to 200 pounds (30 to 90kg).

Okeechobee is good for lake fishing, and big bass are also found in rivers or Lake George. Canals are well stocked and sometimes turn up saltwater fish such as tarpon or snook.

For information on boating and fishing, write to Florida Sports Foundation, 2930 Kerry Forest Parkway, Tallahassee, FL 32309, or look at www.flasports.com. You'll need a visitor's license if you are over 16 and plan to do any fishing, whether saltwater or freshwater. These are available at marinas and tackle shops.

Other Sports

Hiking. Most people stick to walking or jogging along the beaches, but there are plenty of marked trails in national forests and state parks. Only members of the Florida Trail Association may use trails on private property. Membership isn't expensive. Contact: Florida Trail Association Inc., 5415 SW 13th Street, Gainesville, FL 32608, www.floridatrail.org.

Golf. There are over 1,000 golf courses in the state of Florida (see www.floridagolfing.com) – over 40 courses in Greater Miami alone, plus a heavy concentration up the Gold Coast, the Gulf Coast, and in the center and the north of Florida. Some holiday companies offer packages including green fees, but even the regular prices are reasonable, especially if you start after 3pm. If you haven't brought your equipment, clubs and even shoes are for rent at some courses. You may be required to hire and use a ride-on buggy (and to heed warnings not to run over any alligators). Local chambers of commerce will supply lists of courses.

Resort courses have plenty of staff who need tipping, so they won't let you carry your clubs at all. Avoid playing at midday in summer. Rates are lower in summer when the crowds have gone.

Tennis. Many larger hotels have courts; some resorts have teaching facilities and organize tournaments. Miami Beach has nearly 50 courts in two separate tennis centers. Walt Disney World's Contemporary Resort has a tennis clinic with video equipment, practice lanes, and automatic ball machines. Anywhere in Florida you won't be far from a tennis club, but in summer it's best to play in the early morning or late afternoon, avoiding the combination of hot sun and humidity.

Spectator Sports

The climate makes the state ideal for northern **baseball** teams to keep fit during the winter. The Atlanta Braves, Boston Red Sox, Baltimore Orioles, and many others play spring training games in several Florida cities (www.florida grapefruitleague.com). The state has also welcomed a recent influx of professional sports teams. Florida boasts two baseball teams, the Marlins in Miami and the Tampa Bay Rays (www.mlb.com), professional ice-hockey teams in Miami and Tampa (www.nhl.com) and pro basketball's Miami Heat and Orlando Magic (www.nba.com).

In **football**, Miami has its famous Dolphins, who play at Pro Player Stadium (home of the Marlins). Tampa Bay is the base of the Buccaneers and Jacksonville is home of the Jaguars (www.nfl.com). Miami's huge **Orange Bowl** is home to the University of Miami Hurricanes, and on New Year's Day each year two top college teams meet in the Orange Bowl Classic.

Florida hosts some major **tennis** tournaments, notably the Sony Ericsson Open in Miami.

As for professional **golf**, the Honda Classic is held in Palm Beach Gardens every February or March, the Players Championship at Ponte Vedra in May and the World Golf Championships in Miami in March. Also in March is Orlando's Arnold Palmer Invitational.

Horse racing takes place at Calder Race Course just north of Miami, Gulfstream Park at Hallandale, Florida Downs at Tampa (January to mid-March), and Gator

Spring training

Baseball's spring training has been a winter tradition in Florida for nearly 100 years. Today, this practice season has 18 teams playing in 17 cities from mid-February to early April. You can learn more at www.springtraining magazine.com/team.html.

Dan Marino brought glamour to the Dolphins, but no trophies

Down, Pompano, which also has harness racing *(see the local press for details.)* **Greyhound racing** venues include Daytona, Hollywood, Key West, Miami, Orlando, and St Petersburg. If you prefer a more rarefied entertainment, **polo** is a popular winter sport at Palm Beach and Boca Raton.

Most intriguing to a visitor is the action-packed Basque game of *jai alai* (pronounced 'high ligh'). You'll see it played at night in season at the Miami Fronton (3500 NW 37th Avenue), and at Dania, Daytona, Orlando, Fort Pierce, and Orange Lake. Tickets are cheap, because the idea is to get you in to bet on the *parimutuel* (tote) system, which also runs the gambling at the dog and horse races.

Finally, **cars** and **motorbikes** race at Daytona International Speedway. In February, thousands gather for the famous Daytona 500, and the Central Florida town of Sebring stages its 12-hour international sports-car race every March.

SHOPPING

Prices vary enormously from store to store. A swimsuit bought at a seafront hotel boutique may be four times the cost of an identical one in a discount store down the road. Even better bargains are found at the sales that most stores hold several times a year, usually after Christmas, the Fourth of July, and other holidays. A sales tax of around 6.5 percent is added to the ticket price of all purchases.

When and Where to Shop

Hours vary: Suburban malls are open seven days a week, Mon–Sat 10am–9pm, Sun noon–6pm, while shops in city centers are generally open only until around 5.30pm, closing on Sundays. Large chain stores close only for national holidays – and not even all of them. In addition to the shopping centers, supermarkets, specialty shops, discount, and chain stores, Florida has a style of shopping found only in the world's prosperous places: prestige malls. The very buildings reflect the wares within. Featuring tropical landscaping, modern sculpture, and fountains, they are often innovatively designed by creative architects. Inside, the best of American designer boutiques, antiques, and jewelry shops alternate with branches of famous European fashion houses. Even if the prices are out of your league, there's nothing to stop you from window-shopping. Bargain outlet malls abound in Florida. Two of the biggest and best are the outlet malls on north International Drive in Orlando, and Sawgrass Mills near Fort Lauderdale, which calls itself the world's largest outlet center, with over 300 stores.

Check it out...

When shopping at the big outlet malls, it's good to know suggested retail prices, as their advertised bargains aren't always what they seem.

What to Buy

Florida keeps its eyes on Europe, New York, and California, and responds to fashion with the latest in **leisurewear**, robes, swimsuits, and shoes.

'Western stores' sell **cowboy clothes** and leather goods. Florida is a cattle state, so the stores actually supply real cowboys and ranchers, not just tourists, though the merchandise these days is not always made in the United States. A well-fitting pair of cowboy boots will last for years.

Some stores stock **Indian crafts** from all over America, including fine woven

Fancy shopping mall in Naples

blankets, ponchos, wall hangings, and skirts. The local Seminoles specialize in patchwork children's clothing. You can bargain for semi-precious jewelry, often turquoise stones set in silverwork, and artistic pottery. The prices may seem a bit high – they've risen considerably in recent years.

It might seem strange to come here and buy oriental and Asian goods, but the import stores have bargains in woven raffia, wood, leather, wicker furniture, and rugs.

Sports enthusiasts should check out the equipment on sale, especially for golf, tennis, and fishing.

And finally, you can send back a box of Florida sunshine. The larger roadside stands will pack their own tangerines, oranges, or grapefruits and ship them home for you.

ENTERTAINMENT

In downtown **Miami**, concentrated in Little Havana, the dominant note is Cuban, the exiles showing what, for better or worse, the old country was like before the revolution. Supper-clubs and *discotecas* raise the temperature with the latest merengue, salsa, and cumbia sounds. The choice widens in **Miami Beach**, especially along trendy Ocean Drive and Washington Avenue in South Beach, where bars and restaurants feature live jazz, and clubs come and go with bewildering speed. Rock, reggae, 1960s revival, gay clubs, British and Irish pubs – any excuse for drinking and dancing will do.

Theme parks have learned to entertain adults too

The scene is just as varied in **Coconut Grove**. On Friday and Saturday nights you will think everyone in Miami has come here to cruise the streets and pack the bars. Music blares from cars and cafés until the small hours, and street performers entertain crowds of onlookers. If you prefer entertainment a little on the sedate side, Miami and the Beach also have dozens of piano bars. Some agencies organize tours of the nightclubs in a package that includes cocktails at one and dinner at another, sometimes followed by a show.

At **Orlando**, Walt Disney World Resort tries its best to keep guests on site for the evenings at Downtown Disney's Pleasure Island and West Side, with clubs offering everything from comedy to jazz and country and western. And Universal Studios CityWalk has clubs that range from reggae to blues.

Themed dinner-show packages in the Orlando area include 'Arabian Nights' (with as many as 60 horses; www.arabiannights.com), 'Sleuth Mystery Dinner Show' (www.sleuths.com), Pirate's Dinner Adventure (www.piratesdinneradventure.com), and 'Medieval Times' (www.medievaltimes.com), where guests watch jousts while supping on chicken or steak.

Theater, Concerts, Opera, and Ballet

Broadway sends touring shows to Miami, Palm Beach, Fort Lauderdale, Sarasota, Tampa, and Orlando. That American institution, the dinner-theater, where you can get a meal and a play, is available in a dwindling number of cities.

Classical and rock concerts take place year-round in **Miami** at the Gusman Center for the Performing Arts, and the Knight Center across from Du Pont Plaza. Miami-Dade County Auditorium (2901 West Flagler Street) is the venue for the winter seasons of Greater Miami Opera. The Miami City Ballet performs at Jackie Gleason Theater of the Performing Arts on Miami Beach, and the New World Symphony at the Lincoln Theatre on Lincoln Road.

Sarasota declares itself to be the cultural capital of the state and backs up the claim with concerts, ballet, opera, and theater performances at the Van Wezel Hall and at the Ringling Museum's Asolo Repertory Theatre.

Key West specializes in casual live music in its bars and cafés. The Tennessee Williams Fine Arts Center, as its name might suggest, offers drama a little more demanding than the musical comedies up the coast.

CHILDREN'S FLORIDA

There should be no real problem keeping children happy, whether at the many and varied theme parks or on the beaches (the Gulf Coast generally has calmer water and safe, gently sloping sands).

Simple beach resorts are ideal for parents with young children. School-age kids revel in attractions created for their enjoyment, especially the theme park. Florida cities like Miami can be great fun for elementary-age children.

Nearly every hotel and motel in the state has a swimming pool, and the beaches guarantee a day of fun. However, the sun, heat, and humidity can quickly take their toll on youngsters, especially in the form of dehydration, so make sure your children get plenty to drink and use a high-factor sunscreen at all times.

Oh the place you will go! There is fun to be done!

Calendar of Events

January
Greek Festival (Tarpon Springs)
Art Deco Weekend Festival (Miami Beach)

February
Gasparilla Pirate Invasion and Parade (Tampa)
Silver Spurs Rodeo (Kissimmee). A semi-annual fair with calf-roping, steer-wrestling, and other cowboy feats.
Bike Week (Daytona Beach). More than 500,000 motorcycle enthusiasts attend, with parades, shows, and entertainment.

March
Miami International Film Festival
Carnival Miami/Calle Ocho (Miami). Nation's largest Hispanic celebration, culminating in the Calle Ocho Festival.

May
Shrimp Festival (Fernandina Beach)

July
Pepsi 400 (Daytona Beach). Car-racing competition.
Hemingway Days Festival (Key West)

September
Taste of 30-A (Panhandle). Southern cuisine tour among picturesque towns like WaterColor and WaterSound Beach.

October
Fantasy Fest (Key West). Caribbean carnival revelry, zany fun.

November
Sarasota Medieval Fair (Sarasota). On the grounds of the Ringling Museum of Art. Jousting, human chess games, bawdy fun.

December/January
Orange Bowl Festival (Miami). Highlight is the Orange Bowl Parade on New Year's Eve.
British Night Watch and Grand Illumination (St Augustine). Military re-enactments, a candlelit parade, and carol singing commemorate the British period of St Augustine's history and usher in the Christmas period.

EATING OUT

Your eating options are as varied as the peoples that make up Florida – and then some: Italian, Spanish, Mexican, Chinese, Thai, Vietnamese, Japanese, Greek, French – even British pubs serving fish and chips. Cuban cooking prevails in much of Miami alongside Haitian and other Caribbean cuisines, and the Jewish community has brought the best of delicatessen food from New York. And remember, this is part of the South, so you'll be offered grits (similar to semolina). In northern Florida you'll see hog jowls and collard greens in the supermarkets, and boiled peanuts at roadside stalls – a gastronomic trip for the adventurous.

When to Eat

You'll find some places are even open round the clock. Breakfast is served from 6 or 7 to 11am, lunch from about 11.30am to 1.30pm, and dinner from 5 or 6 until 9 or 10pm. Brunch is featured on Sundays between 11am and 3pm. Some restaurants offer an 'early-bird special,' dinner at a lower price if you order before 5 or 6pm.

What to Eat

Fierce competition has resulted in amazing bargains at the lower end of the price range – fast-food, ethnic, and 'family' restaurants, and the all-you-can-eat buffets are usually very good value. A more elegant meal will cost from twice to 10 times as much. Seek local advice – hotel staff are often experts and free with their opinions *(see Recommended Restaurants on page 136).*

Delicatessen restaurants. These specialize in gargantuan sandwiches of corned beef, smoked turkey, roast beef, and many other fillings. Cream cheese and smoked salmon on a bagel is another specialty, as are chopped liver and pastrami.

Takeouts. As well as fast-food outlets, the delicatessens in the better supermarkets are a great place to pick up a **picnic**.

Breakfast. A continental breakfast comprises juice, coffee, and toast or a sweet pastry. Eggs appear on every menu, along with bacon, grits, and sausages, french toast, waffles, and pancakes. European visitors may find American coffee rather weak. If you crave more flavor, find a Cuban snack bar or coffee stall and drink little cups of aromatic *café cubano. Buche* is the strong, black espresso variety.

Soups. You can almost make a meal of thick and filling seafood bisque, navy bean, or Cuban black-bean soup. Conch chowder, a delicious specialty of the Florida Keys, is made from milk, potatoes, vegetables, spices, and chopped conch, a type of shellfish.

News Café in Miami

Salads. Many restaurants offer self-service salad bars. Otherwise, a salad frequently comes with the main course. Chef's salad is a meal in itself, made with lettuce, cheese, ham, turkey, or other cold meats.

Seafood. Florida's fish and shellfish include red snapper, yellowtail, grouper, jumbo shrimp, stone crab, crawfish (aka Florida lobster), and oysters. Don't be afraid to order

Florida Gold

The state's vast citrus groves make it the world's biggest producer of many varieties. Growers large and small have assortments packed ready to send off as soon as an order is received. Here are some of the most popular varieties:

Navel oranges. Easy to peel, thin-skinned and juicy, navels are in season in November.

Temple oranges. Richer in flavor than navels, temples peel like a tangerine – and are virtually seedless.

Valencia oranges. Late-ripeners, Valencias appear at the fruit stands from March to May. They're particularly tasty in fruit salads.

Tangerines. Robinson tangerines ripen in October and November. In December and January you'll find the Dancy variety; in March, the extra-sweet Honey tangerines.

Tangelos. A Florida hybrid, tangelos combine the easy-eating qualities of the tangerine with the flavor of a sweet grapefruit.

Grapefruit. From the Indian River district, Marsh Whites have a nobler, austere acidity; Ruby Reds are sweeter.

Pomelos. Like a bigger, coarser, sweeter grapefruit.

Kumquats. Farmers often give away these little treats, which look like miniature oval oranges. You eat the whole thing, sweet rind and all. Ask for some when you buy fruit.

Limes. Put an aromatic slice of green lime in your gin and tonic and you'll never go back to lemon.

Crab claws have a devoted following

dolphin – it's not the friendly mammal but a tasty fish. Some restaurants avoid confusion by using its Hawaiian name, 'mahi-mahi.'

Stone crab claws, a seasonal delicacy, have a devoted following. Diners don bibs to eat the meat, extracting it from the claws with the aid of a nutcracker and dipping it into a lemon-and-butter or mustard-and-mayonnaise sauce.

You may get a taste for conch fritters (deep-fried pieces of the shellfish), especially on the Keys. Fish is often served with hush puppies (not shoes, but fried cornmeal balls).

Meats. Most Cuban restaurants offer *picadillo* (marinated ground beef mixed with olives, green peppers, garlic, onions, and tomato sauce) and *arroz con pollo* (chicken and rice). A popular dish is an *enchilada*, a tortilla (cornmeal pancake) stuffed with meat, beans, or cheese and baked.

Desserts. Sweet, creamy Key lime pie turns up everywhere in Florida, but especially on the Keys.

Drinks. Fresh fruit juices are excellent, iced water is almost universal and iced tea is an American specialty.

American beer is comparable to European lager, but many imports are available. 'Light' (or 'Lite') doesn't mean low alcohol here, just lower calories. House wines come by the bottle, carafe, or glass. Some restaurants have no license to sell wine, but won't mind if you bring your own bottle. The waiter will open it and provide glasses for a small charge.

Cocktails are served by the glass or, more economically, by the pitcher. The piña colada combines rum, pineapple juice, and coconut milk. Daiquiris are made with rum and

Mojito cocktail at a restaurant in Key West

an assortment of fruit juices – peach, strawberry, or banana, for example. Mimosa is champagne and orange juice, a margarita is a mixture of fresh lime juice, tequila, and ice, and a mojito mixes rum, sugar, lime, carbonated water and mint.

Liquor laws are strictly enforced. You can buy beer and wine in many stores, but spirits are sold only in liquor stores. Cans and bottles of alcohol must not be displayed in public places, but kept in bags at all times. Alcohol is prohibited on many beaches, and no one under 21 years of age is permitted to drink alcohol. You may be asked for an identification document showing your date of birth.

HANDY TRAVEL TIPS

An A–Z Summary of Practical Information

A

ACCOMMODATIONS

(see also RECOMMENDED HOTELS on page 127 and CAMPING)

Florida offers a huge variety of accommodations in every price range. However, in high season reservations may be hard to come by, especially at Walt Disney World Resort and in popular beach resorts. Book well in advance; even a year may not be too much for the Christmas and Easter holidays.

American hotels and motels usually charge by the room, not the number of occupants unless your party is larger than four, but hard-sell advertising may quote a per person rate. State and local taxes, as high as 12 or 13 percent, are added to the bill *(see page 127)*. Most rooms have two double beds, a private bathroom (a shower in smaller motels), and color TV. There may be a refrigerator or mini-bar and cooking facilities.

Efficiencies are small apartments with a kitchenette or separate kitchen and dining area. Facilities usually include dishes, pans, and cutlery. In recent years, tour operators have been offering more and more self-catering villas and apartments to cater for families.

In coastal areas, the farther from the beach you go, the lower the rates should be. Rooms facing a pool or garden are often two-thirds the price of rooms with an ocean view.

High season in Florida is from December 15 to March or April (including Easter). Quietest times are in May and early June and between September and November, when prices are generally lower.

Larger hotels employ a concierge/bell captain who can arrange tours, call a cab, or rent a car for you, but you may be able to economize by making your own arrangements.

AIRPORTS

Miami International Airport (MIA, www.miami-airport.com) is a crowded and confusing place, just west of the city center. Served by about 100 airlines, it's one of the world's busiest airports, with two terminals connected by an automated people-mover. The main terminal, divided into concourses (or zones), has two floors, the lower level for arrivals and baggage claim and the upper for departures and ticketing. Here you'll find bars, fast-food restaurants, telephones, shops, and an information desk open 24 hours a day. If you're not well supplied with dollars, change money at one of the exchange counters. It's unwise to go into town without sufficient US currency, as bureaux de change can be hard to find outside the airport (see MONEY MATTERS).

Orlando International Airport (MCO, www.orlandoairports.net) is spacious, glittering, and constantly expanding. There are two terminals, each with shops, restaurants, and exchange counters. Automatic trains shuttle people to satellite gates. No trolleys are provided, so suitcases with wheels are recommended.

Customs. At both airports, red and green customs channels are in operation, and formalities are generally simple and quick.

Security. In the US airport security is no laughing matter and waits to clear departures can stretch to hours at times of heightened security alerts. Even at quiet times, expect to remove your shoes when walking through scanners and be subject to random, comprehensive searches before boarding the plane. At the time of going to press there are still stingent restrictions regarding on-board luggage which forbids larger quantities of liquids. Check with your airline before departure to prevent any unneccessary delays.

Airlines. The major carriers include Delta www.delta.com, Air Canada www.aircanada.com, US Airways www.usairways.com, American www.americanair.com, Virgin Atlantic www.virginatlantic.com, and British Airways www.british-airways.com.

Ground transport. From Miami International, a taxi to Miami Beach usually takes 15–25 minutes (up to an hour during rush hour). The bright-blue vehicles of the Airport Region Taxi Service (ARTS) carry passengers to nearby destinations for a low flat fare. 'Red Top' minibuses will take you to almost any hotel downtown or on Miami Beach for a third of the taxi fare. Cheaper still are the municipal buses, leaving every 30 to 45 minutes from the main terminal's lower level. The Tri-Rail system runs to Gold Coast resorts. From Orlando International, taxis, which are quite expensive, and shuttle minibuses operate to downtown Orlando, International Drive and Walt Disney World Resort, and to Cocoa Beach. Some hotels, including those of Disney World Resort, run free shuttles. A municipal bus also runs to downtown Orlando.

Check-in time. Arrive at least two hours before either domestic or international flights. For flight information, call your airline.

Other Florida airports. Fort Lauderdale, West Palm Beach, Key West, and Tampa have their own international airports, and several other cities are served by domestic flights.

Domestic flights. Air travel is by far the quickest and most convenient way of getting round the US. A few of the most-traveled routes have shuttle services. Fares change constantly, so it is wise to consult a travel agent, or a website such as www.expedia.com, for the latest information about special deals.

B

BICYCLE RENTAL

Beach resorts have shops that rent bicycles by the hour, day, or week. Some Bed and Breakfast establishments will be happy to provide you with a bicycle. Bikes are an ideal way to get around Key West, for example, with its parking problems and short distances. There are few cycle tracks (Coconut Grove is an exception). Make sure a bicycle lock is included, and check on insurance against theft.

BUDGETING FOR YOUR TRIP

To give you an idea of what to expect, here's a list of average prices. However, they must be taken as broad guidelines, as inflation gradually pushes prices upwards.

Airport transfer. Taxi from Miami International Airport to downtown Miami $30–50; to Miami Beach up to $65. Super Shuttle $15–20, depending on destination.

Taxi from Orlando International Airport to International Drive $30; to Walt Disney World $60.

Babysitters. $4–5 per hour for one or two children, plus transport expenses. Hotels charge $8–10 per hour.

Bicycle rental. $3 per hour; $5–15 per day; $20–35 per week.

Campground. $8–35 per day, per site.

Car rental. Prices vary widely with the company and the season, and depend on what insurance is included. A typical price for a mid-size car with unlimited mileage, fully insured, high season might be $42 per day, $175 per week.

Diving. Half-day from boat with equipment $57; lessons $100/day.

Dry-cleaning. Jacket $4.50 and up; trousers $2.50 and up; dress $6 and up.

Entertainment. Cinema $6–12; nightclub/discotheque $5–20 cover charge, $4–6 drinks; dinner show $30–75.

Gasoline (petrol). As much as $4 per US gallon (approx. 4 liters).

Golf. $25–160 (including cart).

Hairdressers. Man's haircut $7–25; Woman's haircut $15–35; cut, shampoo and set $17–50; coloring $20–60.

Hotels. Double room with bath: deluxe $150 and up; medium price $80–150; budget and motels $60–80. There are big seasonal variations.

Laundry. Shirt $1.75; blouse $3.75.

Meals and drinks. Continental breakfast $4–6; full breakfast $6–10; lunch in snack bar $5–10; in restaurant $8–14; dinner $15–30 (more with entertainment); fast-food meal $3–5; coffee $2; beer $2.50–3.50; glass of wine $3–5; carafe $6–10; bottle $10–20; cocktail $4–6.

Museums. $6–12.

Swamp airboat rides. Approx. $10 (45 minutes); glass-bottom boat approx. $20.

Taxis. Meters start at $1.85, then $2.25 per mile in Miami.

Theme parks. Busch Gardens $67.95; Kennedy Space Center, $38; Parrot Jungle $25.95; SeaWorld $69.95; Wet 'n' Wild $41.95; Universal Studios $73. All are plus tax.

Walt Disney World. One-day ticket (Magic Kingdom, Epcot, Disney-MGM Studios or Animal Kingdom) adult $75, child 3–9 $63; four-day Park Hopper (all parks) adult $269, child $234.

C

CAMPING

Camping in America generally involves recreational vehicles (RVs) – campers, motor homes, or trailers (caravans). If you are camping the American way, the *Rand McNally Campground and Trailer Park Guide* or the voluminous *Woodalls* lists and grades campgrounds according to their facilities. (A 'campsite' in the US means the actual spot where you put your RV or tent.) The *Florida State Parks Guide,* a map of all the excellent state parks and state recreational areas with camping facilities, is available from:

The Florida Department of Natural Resources
Bureau of Education and Information
3900 Commonwealth Boulevard
Tallahassee, FL 32399-3000
www.dept.state.fl.us/parks

In each state park, your length of stay is limited to two weeks. To avoid disappointment, reserve a place in advance by telephone.

Camping beside the road – or on private land without permission – is both illegal and unsafe.

CAR RENTAL/HIRE

Hot competition among car-rental (car-hire) companies keeps rates relatively low, and automatic and air-conditioned cars are the norm. If you can pick up and return the car at the same place, try one of the local businesses. If you plan to drop it off in another city, it's best to reserve a car before you get to the US at one of the international companies – it will be cheaper if booked outside the US.

The well-known car-rental agencies (Avis, Hertz, Budget, etc.) charge higher rental rates, but may include insurance costs in the price; small companies, with little or no insurance included in the rates, offer what may sound like fairly expensive insurance coverage. One way or another, you are advised to make sure you have CDW (collision damage waiver), or you will have to pay for some or all of the cost of repairs.

Many inclusive holidays and fly-drive packages promise a 'free car,' but you may have to pay taxes and CDW when you collect it.

Drivers over 25 with a valid driver's license can rent a car. Some agencies make exceptions for 18-year-old drivers paying with a credit card. For tourists from non-English-speaking countries, a translation of the driver's license may be requested, together with the national license itself, or failing this, an International Driving Permit.

Invariably, it is more convenient to pay with a major credit card rather than cash. If you have no card, you must leave a large deposit. Sometimes cash is refused at night and on weekends. To extend your rental, inform the original office, or stop at the nearest branch office.

The quickest way of comparing prices or booking a car is either online or via a company's reservation number.

Avis: www.avis.com; tel: (800) 331-1212
Budget: www.budget.com; tel: (800) 527-0700
Hertz: www.hertz.com; tel: (800) 654-3131

CLIMATE

Most of the year, the weather ranges from warm to hot, but the coasts are cooled by sea breezes. The peak tourist season is winter, when temperatures and rainfall are at their lowest. You may encounter a brief spell of cool weather, especially in the Panhandle, but it is rarely cold enough to interfere with swimming and sunbathing. From June to October it's hot and humid, and you can expect a bit of rain most days, though rarely so persistent as to be troublesome.

Some tourist brochures boast that you'll never need warm clothing, even in the middle of winter, but prudence suggests otherwise. In winter, Atlantic beaches can be very windy, and there may be some rainy days and cold spells. Even in the south temperatures can dip to near freezing for short periods, though many winter days see temperatures in the 80s, especially in South Florida and on the Keys.

Hurricanes occasionally occur. This may be difficult to believe, based on recent evidence, but on average, Florida is hit only one year in seven and only between June and November, so your chance of being in the wrong place at the wrong time is minimal.

CLOTHING

Whenever it's hot or humid, Floridians turn on their air conditioners. These can blow with arctic chill, so don't forget to take a wrap with you when shopping, dining out, or riding in air-conditioned vehicles – including city buses. Winter can bring surprisingly cold spells, so be ready for any eventuality.

In resorts, casual wear is appropriate round the clock – something light, bright, loose, and made of cotton rather than artificial fibers. Palm Beach is an exception, favoring crisp, conservative and – for men – nautical fashions. If you're likely to go swimming often, pack spare swimwear for a rapid change. Other useful items to bring include an umbrella, sunhat, and comfortable shoes for tramping around theme parks or along rocky trails.

CRIME AND SAFETY (see also EMERGENCIES)

Buying and selling illegal drugs is a serious offense. Florida has a large force of undercover officers (plain-clothes police) who are battling to keep drugs out, and the softly, softly approach to drugs used by some European law-enforcement agencies is definitely not the norm set by authorities in Florida.

Most hotels have a safe for valuables. Never leave money, credit cards, check books, etc., in a hotel room, but always in the safe.

In Miami, beware of pickpockets on buses, in lines, crowded stores, and elevators (lifts). The Miami police warn you to drive with windows up and doors locked, especially in areas with numerous traffic lights. Would-be thieves may stage fake accidents or tell you there's something wrong with your car to get you to stop. All belongings should be placed in the trunk (boot) of the car while you are driving.

An unfortunate trend in the Miami area is the increase in violent crimes. Go out after dark in groups, not alone, and avoid carrying large amounts of cash or valuables. Leave your car with the attendant at a restaurant, nightclub, or discotheque, rather than parking it yourself on a dimly lit side street. Use common sense and avoid certain areas, especially Liberty City in northwest Miami. Avoid sightseeing at night in downtown Miami.

CUSTOMS AND ENTRY REQUIREMENTS

Most countries of the EU (including the UK and Ireland), Australia and New Zealand are members of the Visa Waiver Program and their citizens will be able to enter the US for a short stay by simply presenting a valid passport and a return or onward ticket. South Africans and citizens of most other countries do need a visa, which must be applied for from the local embassy prior to departure. Passport requirements can also be confusing, and it is worth checking the Department of State's website http://travel. state.gov or phoning your local embassy to check on the most up-to-date information.

Duty-free allowance. You will be asked to complete a customs declaration form before you arrive in the US. The chart shows what main duty-free items you may take into the US (you must be over 18 to possess tobacco and over 21 to bring in any alcohol) and, when returning home, into your own country.

Into:	Cigarettes	Cigars	Tobacco	Spirits		Wine
US	200	or 50 or	1,350g	1 liter	or	1 liter
Australia	250	or 250g or	250g	2.25 liters	or	2.25 liters
Canada	200	and 50 and	900g	1.1 liters	or	1.1 liters
Eire	200	or 50 or	250g	1 liter	and	2 liters
N. Zealand	200	or 50 or	250g	1.1 liters	and	4.5 liters
S. Africa	400	and 50 and	250g	1 liter	and	2 liters
UK	200	or 50 or	250g	1 liter	and	2 liters

A non-resident may claim, free of duty and taxes, articles up to $100 in value for use as gifts. Plants and foodstuffs are subject to strict control; visitors from abroad may not import fruits, vegetables, or meat products, or liqueur chocolates. Arriving and departing passengers must report any money or checks exceeding a total of $10,000.

D

DRIVING

Drive on the right. In the US, you may turn right after stopping at a red light, provided there is no cross-traffic, you have given way to pedestrians, and there is no sign to the contrary. Front seat belts must be worn, and you must carry your driver's license.

Lane discipline differs from European norms. American drivers tend to stick to one lane, often making no distinction between fast or 'slow' lanes. However, the left lane is usually used to pass cars and to go fast. You may therefore be passed on either side, so don't change lanes without careful checking. In populated areas, the left lane is generally for making left turns only. Don't drink and drive – driving while intoxicated (DWI) may get you locked up.

Expressways (motorways). A national speed limit of 55mph (88km/h) operates on most highways; on expressways in rural areas, the limit is 70mph (112km/h). Other limits, such as 45mph (72km/h), apply where indicated. If you keep up with the flow of traffic, you'll have no problem, but go any faster, and a patrol car may pull you over.

If you have a breakdown on an expressway, pull over on to the right-hand shoulder, tie a handkerchief to the door handle or radio antenna (aerial), raise the hood (bonnet), and wait in the car for assistance. Use the hazard warning lights.

Tolls. Tolls are collected at turnpikes, and at many bridges and causeways, so keep a supply of coins when traveling.

Gas (petrol) and services. Florida's service stations offer several grades of fuel, but the cheapest is adequate for most rental cars. In some areas it is necessary to prepay, especially at night. Some pumps are operated by inserting a credit card. Note that many stations close in the evenings and on Sundays.

Most rental cars in Florida are equipped with air conditioners; if your car is running low on fuel or overheating, turn it off – it's a substantial strain on the engine.

Parking. Florida's famous attractions usually have large and, in most cases, expensive car parks. Most municipal car parks have meters; the coins required and the times of operation are noted on them. Spaces in the streets are indicated by white lines painted on the road. Your car must point in the direction of the flow of traffic, or nose-in when angle-parking. Do not park by a fire hydrant or a yellow or red curb.

Directions. Try to get help planning your route if you don't know the area you are heading for. Don't assume that if you hit the right number street, avenue, or road you can continue to your destination. It may come to a dead end or pass through undesirable places. The expressways are usually the quickest way of crossing big cities.

Detour	Diversion
Divided highway	Dual carriageway
No passing	No overtaking
Railroad crossing	Level crossing
Traffic circle	Roundabout
Yield	Give way

The American Automobile Association offers assistance to members of affiliated organizations abroad. It also provides travel information for the US and can arrange automobile insurance by the month for owner-drivers. Contact the AAA at 1000 AAA Drive, Heathrow, FL 32746-5063; tel: (407) 444-7000; www.aaa.com.

Road signs. Although the US has begun to change over to international road signs, progress is gradual. Some of the terms used may be unfamiliar or confusing.

E

ELECTRICITY

The US uses 110–115 volt, 60-cycle AC. Plugs are small, flat, and two- or three-pronged; foreigners will need an adapter for shavers, etc; but many hotel rooms supply special sockets in bathrooms.

EMBASSIES AND CONSULATES

For countries that do not maintain a consulate in Florida, the nearest embassy or consulate is listed below.

Canada: 200 South Biscayne Boulevard, Suite 1600, Miami, tel: (305) 579-1600.

Ireland: 345 Park Avenue, 17th Floor, New York, tel: (212) 319-2555.

New Zealand: 37 Observatory Circle NW, Washington, DC, tel: (202) 328-4800.

South Africa: 333 East 38th Street, New York, tel: (212) 213-4880.

United Kingdom: Suite 2800 Brickell Bay Office Towers, 1001 Brickell Bay Drive, Miami, tel: (305) 374-1522.

Australia: Suite 108, 2103 Coral Way, Miami, tel: (305) 858-7633.

EMERGENCIES

(see also CRIME AND SAFETY, HEALTH AND MEDICAL CARE and POLICE)

Dial 911, and the operator will ask if you want police, ambulance, or the fire department.

All towns and cities have a 24-hour number to call in case of emergency, if you need a doctor or a dentist. For a doctor in the Miami area, call 547-5757. For a dentist the number is 667-3647.

G

GAY AND LESBIAN TRAVELERS

Gay and lesbian travelers may find a visit to Florida quite paradoxical. A warm reception will be waiting in Key West and Miami. The former is a favourite gay retirement destination and has gay-only hotels, nightclubs, and some drag clubs. Miami's nightlife could not be more gay- and lesbian-friendly. And Disney World has an annual Gay Day. However, visitors will find that attitudes change dramatically once outside these areas; still, discreet couples should find little difficulty regardless of their destination in the state.

GETTING THERE

Because fares and conditions change frequently, it is advisable to consult travel agents for the latest information.

From North America
By air. Miami, Fort Lauderdale, West Palm Beach, Orlando (for Walt Disney World Resort), Tampa, St Petersburg, and Sarasota are easily accessible from the larger US cities, with many non-stop flights offered daily by numerous carriers to major centers. If you do not have a prefered airline, it is best to compare prices via a travel agency or online with a company such as www.expedia.com.

By bus. Florida destinations are linked to all major centers by Greyhound. Fare and destination information can be found at www.greyhound.com, tel: (800) 231-2222.

By rail. Amtrak (www.amtrak.com; tel: 800-872-7245) advertises various bargain fares, including excursion and family fares and packages with hotel and guide included. It runs a car-carrying train between Lorton near Washington, D.C., and Sanford near Orlando.

By car. Travelers coming down the East Coast can take I-95 via Washington and Savannah. The shortest route from the west is I-10, passing Tucson, El Paso, Houston, and Mobile.

From the UK

By air. There are several daily non-stop flights from Heathrow and Gatwick to Miami, as well as Orlando. There are also direct flights between Orlando and Manchester with Virgin Atlantic.

From other European cities

Non-stop flights operate from Frankfurt, Düsseldorf, and Amsterdam to Orlando and from Amsterdam, Frankfurt, Madrid, Milan, and Paris to Miami. There are many one-stop flights from other cities in Europe.

Fares vary enormously, and it is definitely worth shopping around before booking your flight. In general, the longer ahead you book, the lower the fare, with the exception of stand-by fares which apply only at certain times of year.

Some United States airlines offer travelers from abroad a discount on internal flights, or flat-rate, unlimited-travel tickets for specific periods.

Charter flights and package tours. Most charter flights must be booked and paid for well in advance. Many package tours are available: camper holidays, coach tours, excursions to Walt Disney World Resort, or the Bahamas, trips to other American cities, etc. Most Caribbean cruises originate in Florida ports.

Some two-center holidays divide their time between Orlando and one of the beaches (East or West Coast). Other combinations offer Orlando plus a short cruise or a spell on a Caribbean island.

Baggage. You may check in, free, two suitcases of normal size. One piece of hand luggage which fits under the aircraft seat may also be carried on board. Most liquids, including make-up and drinks, are no longer allowed in carry-on luggage. Confirm size and weight restrictions with your travel agent or airline when booking your ticket.

It is advisable to insure all luggage for the duration of your trip, preferably as part of a general travel insurance policy. Any travel agent can arrange this.

GUIDES AND TOURS

Some of the larger attractions provide the services of a guide for a charge. At Walt Disney World's Magic Kingdom, for example, ask at the Town Hall. Foreign-language guides are on call to take visitors on a quick tour, including a selection of rides.

Sightseeing tours by bus or tram are available in most cities. One-day tours from Miami to Disney World Resort are not recommended – they don't allow enough time once you get there.

Pleasure cruises operate from many resorts, touring the coast, the inlets, lakes, rivers, and swamps, some serving meals on board or stopping at a restaurant. Miami and Miami Beach are well served, with tours and cruises up and down the coast. At Key Largo you can take a glass-bottomed boat to view the coral reefs. Tours and cruises are also available in Fort Lauderdale, West Palm Beach, St Petersburg, Sarasota, Naples, Tarpon Springs, and Key West.

H

HEALTH AND MEDICAL CARE (see also EMERGENCIES)

Foreigners should note that the US doesn't provide free medical services, and that treatment can be very, very expensive. Arrangements should therefore be made in advance for temporary health insurance via your travel insurance policy; otherwise an ordinary medical procedure could make an enormous dent in your savings or cause you to go into unnecessary debt.

Walk-in clinics offer less prohibitively expensive treatment than private practitioners, but are often overcrowded and well below normal European standards. Emergency rooms of hospitals will treat anyone in need of attention, including hospitalization in a community ward; but if you arrive with a non-life-threatening injury or illness and cannot prove your ability to pay with an insurance policy or other means, you may well be turned away and refused treatment.

If you arrive in Florida after flying through several time zones, take it easy the first couple of days. Doctors recommend that visitors eat lightly initially, and get plenty of rest.

Beware of the powerful sun. The best advice is to start with a high protection factor (25 or more) sunscreen or sunblock, and build up a tan gradually in small doses.

Drink plenty of water. It is all too easy to become dehydrated – the warning signs are headaches and weariness.

Visitors from the UK will find that some medicines sold over the counter at home can only be bought on prescription in the US. Additionally-
, prices tend to be higher than in Europe, so you may wish to bring a small stock of needed medication with you. On the bright side, there's no shortage of drugstores, or pharmacies; most of them stay open all night.

HOLIDAYS

If a holiday, such as Independence Day, falls on a Sunday, banks and most stores close on the following day. At long weekends (such as the one following Thanksgiving), offices are closed for four days. Many restaurants never shut, however, even at Christmas.

New Year's Day	**January 1**
Martin Luther King Day	**Third Monday in January**
President's Day	**Third Monday in February**
Memorial Day	**Last Monday in May**

Independence Day	**July 4**
Labor Day	**First Monday in September**
Columbus Day	**Second Monday in October**
Veterans' Day	**November 11**
Thanksgiving Day	**Fourth Thursday in November**
Christmas Day	**December 25**

I

INTERNET ACCESS

Some of Florida's larger resorts offer internet access in their business centers, usually at a rate of a few dollars per hour. If you're bringing a laptop on your trip, many hotels and motels have in-room high-speed Internet service.

There also are a handful of internet cafés in larger cities, although these tend to come and go and can be very difficult to locate. One hint is to look in neighbourhoods that have a large immigrant population.

Several chain cafés and retailers offer free Wi-Fi services, including Starbucks coffee shops, Barnes & Noble, and Borders bookstore.

L

LANGUAGE

Miami is officially a bilingual city, and such has been the influence and quantity of refugees, mainly from Cuba, that you'll hear as much Spanish as English on the streets. Downtown most vendors will begin conversations in Spanish, assuming you will understand.

LAUNDRY

Most larger hotels offer these services, at a price. Some hotels have coin-operated washing machines and dryers. Most Disney resorts, being very family-minded, have laundrettes on their premises that contain coin-operated washing machines and dryers.

M

MAPS

Maps can be purchased in numerous places. Road maps are available at all gas stations, and the local chamber of commerce or tourist authority will give or sell you maps with attractions marked on them. Quite good maps are sometimes given out when you hire a car.

MEDIA

Newspapers and Magazines

Local newspapers and the national daily *USA Today* are sold in drugstores and from vending machines. Special news-stands carry *The New York Times* and the *Wall Street Journal,* as well as a variety of other newspapers. Two daily papers are printed in Miami: the *Miami Herald* (*El Nuevo Miami Herald* in Spanish) and the *Diario Las Américas*. The *Orlando Sentinel* provides information about Central Florida. The *St Petersburg Times* is the largest circulation newspaper in the state. A local paper will put you in touch with community news and list TV programs, opening hours of attractions, grocery-store bargains, etc.

Most Florida cities have their own magazines with articles on events. Look for free ones in hotel lobbies.

Radio and TV

Numerous AM and FM radio stations broadcast pop, rock, and country and western music; most large cities also have a classical station. Local AM talk shows are a good barometer of regional politics and can also be very entertaining for their extreme views and gregarious hosts. National Public Radio (NPR) is a US station similar to the BBC World Service or Radio 4 and concentrates on documentaries and discussion shows with some plays. It has several affiliate stations in Florida. Check its website at www.npr.org to find the one nearest you. The World Service's affiliates can be found at www.bbc.co.uk/worldservice.

Almost every hotel room has a television carrying many channels, some 24 hours a day. Local news begins around 6pm, with national and international news from 6.30 or 7pm.

MONEY MATTERS

Currency. The dollar is divided into 100 cents. Banknotes include $1, $2 (rare), $5, $10, $20, $50, and $100. All notes, except the new $100 bills, are the same size and color, so beware of mixing them up. Coins include 1¢ (called a 'penny'), 5¢ ('nickel'), 10¢ ('dime'), 25¢ ('quarter'), 50¢ ('half dollar'), and $1. Only the first four are commonly used.

Banks and currency exchange. Banking hours are usually from 9am to 4pm, Monday to Friday, but take note that very few banks change foreign currency. Walt Disney World's banks are a notable exception. Even in major cities, there may be only one counter in one bank able to handle foreign money. American hotel receptionists tend to be distrustful of foreign banknotes, and they may offer a low exchange rate (so be aware of the exact rate before changing any money). It is simpler to carry US dollar traveler's checks, major credit cards, and just change your cash to dollars before leaving your home country. Most European bank cards will work in US automatic teller machines (ATMs), so you could also just withdraw money as needed after your arrival. It's wise to check the exchange rates and charges on all your bank cards before using them abroad. Some card companies charge prohibitive fees for this service.

When changing money or traveler's checks, ask for $20 bills, which are accepted everywhere, as some establishments will refuse larger notes unless they nearly equal the amount to be paid.

Credit cards. When shopping or paying hotel bills, you may be asked: 'Cash or charge?' meaning you have the choice of paying in cash or by credit card. Businesses are wary of little-known cards, but most accept the top American or international cards. You'll often need some form of identification when charging your purchase.

Many service stations and other businesses will not take money at night, only cards. Outside normal office hours, it's sometimes impossible to rent cars and pay bills with cash.

Traveler's checks. These are safer than cash. They can quickly be exchanged as long as they are in US dollars. Banks will usually want to see your passport or other form of ID, but many hotels, shops, and restaurants will accept them directly in lieu of cash, especially those issued by American banks. Change only small amounts at a time: keep the balance of your checks in your hotel safe if possible and make a note of serial numbers, and where and when you used each check.

Prices. Most displayed prices do not include a sales tax of 6–7 percent – it's added when you pay. The same applies to your hotel bill, which may be further increased by local taxes.

Prices vary considerably in Florida. For moderately priced goods, visit the big department or discount stores. Small independent grocery stores, drugstores, and 24-hour convenience stores have larger mark-ups.

O

OPENING HOURS

Most shops and businesses are open from 8 or 9am (shopping malls from 9.30 or 10am) to 5pm or later. Some stores and chain restaurants never close. Restaurants usually close by 11pm.

P

POLICE

City police are concerned with local crime and traffic violations, while Highway Patrol officers (also called State Troopers) ensure highway safety, and are on the lookout for people speeding or driving under the influence of alcohol or drugs. For emergencies, dial 911 (fire, police, and ambulance).

POST OFFICES

The US postal service deals only with mail; telephone and telegraph services are operated by other companies. Mail letters in the blue curbside boxes. You can buy stamps from machines in post office entrance halls after hours. Stamps from machines in hotels and shops cost a lot more than face value.

Post office hours are from 8am to 5pm Monday to Friday, and from 8am to 12 noon on Saturdays. In larger towns, one branch usually remains open later in the evening, until 9pm or so.

PUBLIC TRANSPORTATION
(see also AIRPORTS, GETTING THERE, CAR RENTAL/HIRE, and DRIVING)

Buses. (See also GUIDES AND TOURS.) The largest company, Greyhound Lines www.greyhound.com serves all major resorts and attractions. As well as the Florida network, it offers services to and from cities all over the US (New York to Orlando takes around 25 hours.) Smaller bus lines provide local shuttle services between hotels and attractions, as well as sightseeing tours. Visitors can buy unlimited rover passes (these can only be bought outside the US), valid for a specified length of time, to go anywhere in the country by Greyhound bus at a flat rate.

City buses. You must have the exact change ready to deposit in the box beside the driver. Miami buses can be crowded and frantic, but, generally speaking, service is regular and punctual.

Miami Metrorail. Miami has an elevated railway running through the center of the city. The air-conditioned trains operate at frequent intervals from 5.30am to midnight.

Taxis. Taxis always carry a roof sign and can easily be recognized. Most have meters, and the rates are generally marked on the doors.

Some cruise the streets, especially in city centers. To phone for a taxi, look in the *Yellow Pages* under 'Taxicabs.' Tip 15 percent.

Trains. Amtrak (National Railroad Passenger Corporation, www.amtrak.com), offers a variety of bargain fares, including excursion and family fares; the USA Railpass can only be purchased abroad, but many package tours are available in the US. Air-conditioned trains link Florida's main towns with urban centers throughout the US (New York to Orlando takes 24 hours.) The Tri-Rail (www.tri-rail.com) system connects Miami and the international airport with Gold Coast cities and resorts.

R

RELIGION

Saturday newspapers often list the church services of the following day, with details of visiting preachers. Besides Catholic, Episcopalian, Presbyterian, and Methodist churches there are many Southern Baptist denominations. In Miami Beach and along the Gold Coast there are numerous synagogues, and there's at least one in every main town.

T

TELEPHONES

When dialing from abroad, the country code for the US is 1. Major city area codes include: Miami – **305**, **786**; Orlando – **407**, **321**; Fort Lauderdale – **754**, **954**; St Petersburg – **727**; and Tampa – **813**. American telephone companies are efficient and reliable. Dialing directions are always posted beside public telephones.

Telephone rates are listed in the introduction to the white pages of the telephone directory, along with information on personal (person-to-person), reverse-charge (collect), and credit-card calls. All numbers with an 800, 888, 877, 866, or 855 prefix are toll-free.

Local calls cost 50¢ for an unlimited amount of time. Hotels add hefty surcharges to all outgoing calls.

Local calls. Lift the receiver, deposit the coins in the slot, wait for the dial tone, then dial the seven- or ten-digit number. The operator will automatically inform you of any additional charge, so have some change ready. For local directory inquiries, dial 411. For local operator assistance, and for help within the same area code, dial 0.

Long-distance calls may be dialed direct from a pay phone if you follow the posted directions. The prefix 1 usually has to be dialed before the number. If you don't know the correct area code, dial 0 for operator assistance. Long-distance calls cost more from a pay phone than from a private one, unless it's a hotel phone which will charge extortionate rates for long-distance calls, even short ones. For international direct-dial calls, dial the prefix 011 followed by the country code and the telephone number.

Phone cards are available for sale at all service stations and supermarkets, as well as newsstands and drug stores, and allow you to prepay for long-distance calls at a much reduced rate. You can make your call from any phone by dialing the designated toll-free number. Do check with your hotel first – some less scrupulous establishments will administer a costly service charge for dialing toll-free numbers.

Fax. You can send faxes from many hotels, and from office-service bureaux found in some shopping malls.

Telegrams. American telegraph companies offer domestic and overseas services, as well as telex facilities, and are listed in the *Yellow Pages*. You can telephone the telegraph office, dictate the message, and have the charge added to your hotel bill, or dictate it from a coin-operated phone and pay on the spot. A letter telegram (night letter) costs about half the rate of a normal telegram. Note the UK does not have a telegram service; your message will be delivered with the mail.

TIME ZONES

The continental US has four time zones; Florida (like New York City) is on Eastern Standard Time except for part of the Panhandle that is on Central Time. Between March and November, Daylight Saving Time is adopted and clocks move ahead one hour. The following chart shows the time in various cities in winter when it's noon in Florida:

Los Angeles	**Miami**	London	Sydney
9am	**noon**	5pm	4am

TIPPING

Waiters and waitresses earn most of their salary from tips; often they are paid little else. In simple eating houses you usually pay the cashier on your way out, after leaving a tip on the table. Otherwise, you can write in the tip on a credit-card slip: they always leave a space for it.

Some suggestions:

Guide	10–15 percent
Hairdresser/barber	15 percent
Hotel porter (per bag)	50¢–$1 (minimum total $1)
Taxi driver	15 percent
Waiter	15–20 percent (unless service has been added to the bill)

TOILETS

You can find toilets in restaurants, railway stations, and large stores, as well as hotels and restaurants. In some places you must deposit a coin, in others you can leave a tip for the attendant if there is one.

Americans use the terms 'restroom,' 'powder room,' 'bathroom,' (private), and 'ladies' room' or 'men's room' to indicate the toilet.

TOURIST INFORMATION

Information for travel to Florida is handled by **Visit Florida**, which maintains offices in the state and abroad. Details are below.

In the UK you can request a brochure by phoning (0870) 770-1177 or visiting www.visitflorida.com.

In the US: **Visit Florida**, PO Box 1100, Tallahassee, FL 32302-1100, tel: (888) 735-2872.

There are also five official Florida Welcome Centers, which are on I-95, I-10, I-75, and US231 near the state borders and at the Capitol building in Tallahassee.

TRAVELERS WITH DISABILITIES

More efforts have been made in the United States than almost any other country to enable those with physical disabilities to get around. Hotels and public buildings have wheelchair entrances and special toilets. Theme parks make as many of their attractions as possible accessible to wheelchairs, and some provide special help to sight- and hearing-impaired visitors.

WEBSITES

There are dozens of helpful websites for Florida destinations. Here are sites for major destinations and each of the geographical regions of the state:

Official Visit Florida website	**www.visitflorida.com**
State parks	**www.dep.state.fl.us/parks**
Historical sites	**www.flheritage.com**
Florida Panhandle beaches	**www.destin-ation.com**
	www.beachesofsouthwalton.com
North Central Florida	**www.originalflorida.org**
Northeast Florida/	**www.ameliaisland.org**
St Augustine	**www.oldcity.com**

Central East Florida	**www.space-coast.com**
	www.daytonabeach.com
Orlando	**www.orlandoinfo.com**
Central West Florida	**www.sarasotafl.org**
	www.floridasbeach.com
	www.tampabay.com
Southwest Florida	**www.fortmyers-sanibel.com**
	www.sanibel-captiva.org
Southeast Florida,	**www.palmbeachfl.com**
Miami and The Keys	**www.gmcvb.com**
	www.fla-keys.com
SeaWorld Orlando	**www.seaworld.com**
Walt Disney World Resort	**disneyworld.disney.go.com**
Universal Orlando	**www.universalorlando.com**
Busch Gardens, Tampa Bay	**www.buschgardens.com**

WEIGHTS AND MEASURES

The United States is one of the few countries in the world that has not yet adopted the metric system. It has no plans to do so.

Y

YOUTH HOSTELS

Backpacking is not as easy in the United States as it is in most European countries. There are only about 160 hostels throughout all of the United States, ranging from basic and utilitarian to warm and inviting. Most are located outside the big cities, and the distances between them can be enormous and they are rarely connected via public transportation. Some budget hotels offer a large discount to International YHA (Youth Hostel Association) members. There is no age limit. For information, apply to: Hostelling International-USA, 8401 Colesville Road, Suite 600, Silver Springs, MD 20910, tel: (301) 495-1240, www.hiusa.com.

Recommended Hotels

Long-established and still growing as a holiday destination, Florida offers a huge choice of accommodations. All resorts have representatives of the big chains and franchises, as well as rows of budget motels. The Orlando area, including Walt Disney World Resort, has more hotel rooms than any city in the United States except Las Vegas. Competition in the highly developed hospitality industry means that you'll be assured of value for money, whether you choose the most luxurious resort, a modest motel, or something in between. Here we can only make a small selection. We have subdivided the list by area, following the same order as the Where to Go section of this guide. Each entry is marked with a symbol indicating the price range, per night, for a double room with bath, excluding breakfast. Sales tax (varies from county to county) is added to hotel bills. All take major credit cards unless indicated otherwise.

In the US, rates quoted are for the room, not per person. Additional occupants over two may be charged a small premium. A few places include a simple Continental breakfast. Always ask about special-rate packages, e.g. for stays of a few days, lower mid-week rates, and off-season rates. (Two symbols, e.g. $$–$$$, indicate major seasonal variations between price ranges.)

$$$$	$220 and over
$$$	$120–220
$$	$80–120
$	up to $80

MIAMI BEACH TO AVENTURA

The Albion $$$ *1605 James Ave. at Lincoln Road, Miami Beach, FL 33139, tel: (305) 913-1000 or (877) 782-3557, www.rubell hotels.com.* A classic, nautically-inspired Art Deco hotel dating from 1939, stylishly renovated with minimalist decor and custom wood furnishing and all mod-cons. For some, the rooms may be too cold, for others they will be the height of chic. Outdoor pool, fitness center, bar and restaurant. 96 rooms and suites.

Circa 39 $ *3900 Collins Ave., Miami Beach, FL 33140, tel: (305) 538-4900 or (877) 824-7223, fax: 538-4998, www.circa39.com.* You won't find many better bargains than this landing zone, a bit north of South Beach. The knock: it's on the wrong side of Collins Avenue and, therefore, not on the beach. 82 rooms.

Clay Hotel and International Hostel $–$$ *1438 Washington Ave., Miami Beach, FL 33139, tel: (305) 534-2988 or (800) 379-2529, fax: 673-0346, www.clayhotel.com.* Hostelling International's only location in Miami, this is undoubtedly one of its premier properites. In addition to traditional hostel bunks, many rooms are private and have their own bath and toilet facilities. Located on the corner of Washington Avenue and Spanish-themed Espanola Way. 25 rooms.

Delano Hotel $$$$ *1685 Collins Ave., Miami Beach, FL 33139, tel: (305) 672-2000 or (800) 697-1791, fax: 532-0099, www.delano-hotel.com.* A rooftop spa and poolside cabanas – the pool with soothing underwater music – are part of the attraction of this South Beach hotel, which was the original boutique arrival on the beach. The predominantly white rooms are on the cramped side, but many have stunning ocean views, and the suites have luxurious marble bathrooms. 194 rooms and suites.

Fontainebleau Suites Miami Beach $$$–$$$$ *4441 Collins Ave., Miami Beach, FL 33140, tel: (305) 538-2000 or (800) 548-8886, fax: 674-4607, www.fontainebleau.com.* This historic Miami Beach resort wraps around nearly half a mile of prime oceanfront. Beautiful curving lobby, tree-filled grounds with swimming pool featuring rock grottoes and waterfalls. Wheelchair access. 1,206 rooms.

Loews Miami Beach Hotel $$$ *1601 Collins Ave., Miami Beach, FL 33139, tel: (305) 604-1601 or (800) 235-6397, fax: 604-3999, www.loewshotels.com.* The centerpiece of this luxury oceanfront hotel is the St Moritz Hotel, faithfully restored to its original Art Deco splendor. Pool, superb spa, and fitness center. Wheelchair access. 800 rooms.

MIAMI AREA

Biltmore Hotel $$$$ *1200 Anastasia Ave., Coconut Grove, FL 33134, tel: (305) 445-1926 or (800) 727-1926, fax: 913-3159, www.biltmorehotel.com.* Built by George Merrick in 1926, this is still one of Florida's leading hotels, with every detail steeped in luxury. 275 rooms and suites.

Doubletree $$ *2649 S. Bayshore Drive, Coconut Grove, FL 33133, tel: (305) 858-2500 or (800) 776-1491, fax: 858-5776, www.doubletree.com.* Spacious rooms with views of the bay and the 'Grove.' Pool, tennis. Wheelchair access. 198 rooms.

Ritz-Carlton, Coconut Grove $$$ *3300 SW 21st Ave., Coconut Grove, FL 33133, tel: (305) 644-4680 or (800) 542-8680, fax: 644-4681, www.ritzcarlton.com.* A spa, views of Biscayne Bay, and Ritz's usual first-class amenities make this a favorite of many frequent visitors. 115 rooms and suites.

Sonesta Beach Resort Key Biscayne $$$–$$$$ *350 Ocean Drive, Key Biscayne, FL 33149, tel: (305) 361-2021 or (800) 766-3782, fax: 365-2096, www.sonesta.com.* Every room in the Sonesta has a view of the Atlantic or Key Biscayne; corner rooms overlook both the bay and the ocean. This resort is perfect for families, with free children's programs every day of the week. Fitness center, excellent tennis program, pools, watersports, golf course adjoining. Wheelchair access. 300 rooms.

THE FLORIDA KEYS

Cheeca Lodge $$$$ *MM 82, Overseas Highway, Islamorada, Box 527, FL 33036, tel: (305) 664-4651 or (800) 327-2888, fax: 664-2893, www.cheeca.com.* This informal and beautiful seaside resort is known for the great fishing off the 525ft (160m) lighted pier. Every room has been completely redecorated or is completely new. Golf, tennis, saltwater and freshwater pools, watersports, environmental tours of the Keys, two excellent restaurants. Wheelchair access. 203 rooms.

Jules' Undersea Lodge $$$$ *MM 103.2, 51 Shoreland Drive, Key Largo, FL 33037, tel: (305) 451-2353, fax: 451-4789, www.jul. com.* Scuba enthusiasts love this underwater hotel, located 30ft (9m) beneath the ocean. This two-bedroom underwater cottage includes a well-stocked kitchen, books, music, and videos – and views that beat any TV. Can accommodate up to six.

La Pensione $$–$$$ *809 Truman Ave., Key West, FL 33040, tel: (305) 292-9923 or (800) 893-1193, fax: 296-6509, www.la pensione.com.* Courteous staff, ceiling fans, private baths, and French doors overlooking the verandas give this Bed and Breakfast the island feel of Key West's interior. At breakfast expect Belgian waffles, fresh fruit, breads, and muffins. Wheelchair access. Nine rooms.

SOUTHEAST FLORIDA/THE GOLD COAST

The Breakers $$$–$$$$ *1 S. Country Road, Palm Beach, FL 33480, tel: (561) 655-6611 or (888) 273-2537, fax: 659-8403, www.thebreakers.com.* This massive oceanfront palace dating from the 1920s was recently renovated, adding new oceanfront club and soundproofing rooms. Two golf courses, tennis, croquet, pools. The Sunday brunch is legendary. Wheelchair access. 560 rooms.

Marriott Harbor Beach Resort Spa $$$–$$$$ *3030 Holiday Drive, Fort Lauderdale, FL 33316, tel: (954) 525-4000 or (800) 222-6543, fax: 766-6165, www.marriott.com.* Luxury resort not far from the Fort Lauderdale 'strip,' with balconies on every room – try to get up as high as possible. A boardwalk leads to the beach, but the enormous free-form pool with a waterfall is perfect for sunning. Tennis, watersports, and nearby golf. 622 rooms.

CENTRAL EAST AND NORTHEAST FLORIDA

Amelia Island Plantation $$–$$$$ *1501 Lewis St., Amelia Island, FL 32034, tel: (904) 261-6161 or (888) 261-6161, fax: 277-5159, www.aipfl.com.* Resort and residential community in a lush forest of live oak, magnolia, and pine. Rent a room or a house, all attractively decorated and convenient for a variety of sports like tennis, golf, fishing, boating, and horseback riding. Wheelchair access. 660 rooms.

Disney Vero Beach Resort $$$ *9250 Island Grove Terrace, Vero Beach, FL 32963, tel: (561) 231-1600 or (800) 359-8000, fax: 234-2030, www.disneyvacationclub.com.* This is a great beachfront location for Disney World fans. All of the sumptuously decorated rooms overlook a garden or the ocean; the beach is small and most guests tend to lounge around the giant swimming pool with its spiral slide. Excellent children's programs and family excursions. Wheelchair access. 175 rooms.

The Inn at Summer Bay $$ *25 Town Center Boulevard, Suite C, Clermont, FL 34711, tel: (352) 242-1100, ext. 7417, or (800) 654-6102, fax: 241-2768, www.summerbayresort.com.* These spacious guest rooms come equipped with microwave and refrigerator. Adjacent to Summer Bay Resort with full access to amenities, including a lake with aqua park, volleyball, basketball, boating, and fishing.

Perry's Ocean Edge Resort $–$$$ *2209 S. Atlantic Ave., Daytona Beach, FL 32118, tel: (386) 255-0581 or (800) 447-0002, fax: 258-7315, www.perrysoceanedge.com.* The Perry family has operated this beachfront hotel for more than 50 years, and start each morning cooking fresh donuts for free breakfast for guests. For peace and quiet, ask for a room in the newer towers instead of the old motel. Indoor pool is nice for wet days. Wheelchair access. 204 rooms.

WALT DISNEY WORLD RESORT

Guests in Disney-owned accommodations have privileges in making reservations for shows, dinner, golf, etc., and entry to the parks by Disney transportation is guaranteed. These advantages can offset the somewhat higher prices of rooms within Disney World Resort. The central hotel number for Disney properties is (407) W-DISNEY.

Animal Kingdom Lodge $$$$ *Walt Disney World, Lake Buena Vista, FL 32830, tel: (407) 934-7639, fax: 939-1001, www.disney world.com.* A jungle lodge ambience, views of wildlife grazing on savannahs, and African cuisine are the magnets to this newer Disney deluxe resort. 1,293 rooms.

Disney's All-Star Resorts $–$$ *Walt Disney World, Lake Buena Vista, FL 32830, tel: (407) 934-7639, fax: 939-7111, www.disney world.com.* The best bargain on Disney property, these small, whimsically decorated rooms are themed to movies, music, and sports. Food court, giant pools, and video arcades. Wheelchair access. 5,760 rooms.

Disney's Coronado Springs Resort $$–$$$ *Walt Disney World, Lake Buena Vista, FL 32830-0100, tel: (407) 934-7639, fax: 939-1001, www.disneyworld.com.* Near Disney's Animal Kingdom and Blizzard Beach water park, Coronado has a Southwestern US theme, with three guest areas stretching around a lake. Rooms are smaller than at Disney's deluxe hotels, but comfortable for a family of four. Wheelchair access. 1,967 rooms.

Grand Floridian Resort and Spa $$$$ *Walt Disney World, Lake Buena Vista, FL 32830, tel: (407) 934-7639, fax: 824-3196, www.disneyworld.com.* The crème de la crème of Disney hotels, a re-creation of Victorian splendor with a palatial lobby and luxurious rooms. Monorail to the Magic Kingdom. Pools, marina, beach. 901 rooms.

DISNEY'S HOTEL PLAZA BOULEVARD

Designated 'Hotels of Walt Disney World,' these are inside WDW but not Disney-owned. All are located near Downtown Disney, inexpensive eateries, and a 24-hour grocery store.

Buena Vista Palace $$–$$$$ *1900 Buena Vista Drive, Lake Buena Vista, FL 32830, tel: (407) 827-2727 or (866) 397-6516, fax: 827-6034, www.buenavistapalace.com.* Lakeside towers with three swimming pools, spa, restaurants, and recreation area. Wide variety of rooms and suites to suit every requirement. Wheelchair access. 1,014 rooms.

Doubletree Guest Suites $$$–$$$$ *2305 Hotel Plaza Boulevard, Lake Buena Vista, FL 32830, tel: (407) 934-1000 or (800) 222-8733, fax: 934-1015, www.doubletreehotels.com.* Units are spacious, with a living room and separate bedroom. Heated pool, fitness room, tennis, and children's playground. Wheelchair access. 229 rooms.

ORLANDO AREA

Hyatt Regency Grand Cypress $$$–$$$$ *1 Grand Cypress Blvd., Lake Buena Vista, FL 32836, tel: (407) 239-1234 or (800) 233-1234, fax: 239-3800, www.hyattgrandcypress.com.* Here's a resort that is very near Disney's eastern boundary but buffered by spacious, sometimes wooded grounds. Recreation facilities abound, including a 0.5-acre (0.2 hectares) pool with waterfalls and grottoes. 750 rooms.

Park Plaza $–$$$ *307 Park Ave., Winter Park, FL 32789, tel: (407) 647-1072 or (800) 228-7220, fax: 647-4081, www.parkplaza hotel.com.* Small, lovely hotel in sophisticated Winter Park. Rooms are elegantly appointed with brass beds, oriental rugs, and ceiling fans. Most overlook Park Avenue. The Amtrak train station is just steps away, so night-time trains can wake light sleepers. Wheelchair access. 27 rooms.

Portofino Bay Hotel $$$$ *5601 Universal Blvd., Orlando, FL 32819, tel: (407) 503-1000 or (800) 232-7827, fax: 503-1010, www.universalorlando.com/portofinobay.* Located at Universal Orlando. Amenities here include eight restaurants and lounges, a spa, and two pools. Butler service in some rooms and suites. Wheelchair access. 750 rooms.

Westin Grand Bohemian $$$–$$$$ *325 S. Orange Ave., Orlando, FL 32801, tel: (407) 313-9000 or (866) 663-0024, fax: 313-9001, www.grandbohemianhotel.com.* Upper floors in this smoke-free hotel overlook the pool or downtown Orlando, and all of the rooms have Heavenly Beds with down comforters and pillows. Public areas have 19th- and 20th-century art. Wheelchair access. 250 rooms.

THE EVERGLADES

Everglades City Motel $–$$ *310 Collier Ave. (State Road 29), Everglades City, FL 34139, tel: (239) 695-4224 or (800) 695-8353, www.evergladescitymotel.com.* Located in the heart of Everglades City, rooms are modest but comfortable, with a choice of standard, efficiencies (with stove, microwave, and toaster), or apartments. Guests get discounts at nearby Captain Doug's Small Airboat Tours.

SOUTHWEST FLORIDA

Pink Shell Beach Resort $$$–$$$$ *275 Estero Blvd., Ft. Myers Beach, FL 33931, tel: (239) 463-6181 or (888) 222-7465, fax: 463-1229, www.pinkshell.com.* The Pink Shell Beach Resort has a reputation for some of the most fun activities on the beach. Families flock here, and all rooms are equipped with refrigerators, microwaves, and coffee makers. There are three swimming pools, tennis, bike rentals, boat tours, and a fishing pier. Wheelchair access. 209 rooms.

Ritz-Carlton Hotel $$$–$$$$ *280 Vanderbilt Beach Road, Naples, FL 34108, tel: (239) 598-3300 or (800) 241-3333, fax: 598-6690, www.ritzcarlton.com.* Bet on impeccable service and comfort at the award-winning Ritz. All rooms have a lovely view of the Gulf, and every luxury is at your fingertips – if not, just ask. Pool, watersports, tennis, fitness center, and nearby golf. Wheelchair access. 463 rooms.

'Tween Waters Inn $$–$$$ *15951 Captiva Road, Captiva Island, FL 33924, tel: (239) 472-5161 or (800) 223-5865, fax: 472-0249, www.tween-waters.com* On the narrowest piece of Captiva, this historic inn is quaint and natural, though new condos have been built in place of some of the old cottages. Across the street from the Gulf of Mexico, with plenty of outdoor activities and an uncrowded stretch of beach. Full-service marina. Wheelchair access. 137 rooms.

CENTRAL WEST FLORIDA

Don CeSar Beach Resort and Spa $$$–$$$$ *3400 Gulf Blvd., St Pete Beach, FL 33706-4098, tel: (727) 360-1881 or (800) 235-6397, fax: 367-6952, www.doncesar.com.* This striking pink palace on the beach opened in 1928, and many celebrities have enjoyed the sumptuous surroundings. Guest rooms are spotless. Two heated pools, tennis courts on the beach, watersports. Wheelchair access. 277 rooms.

Holiday Inn Sunspree $$–$$$ *715 S. Gulfview Blvd., Clearwater Beach, FL 33767, tel: (727) 447-9566 or (800) 465-4329, fax: 446-6093, www.hiclearwaterbeach.com.* Dependable chain hotel situated on the southernmost point of Clearwater Beach. Pool, beach playground. Wheelchair access. 205 rooms.

The Resort at Longboat Key Club $$–$$$ *301 Gulf of Mexico Drive, Longboat Key, FL 34228, tel: (941) 383-8821 or (888) 237-5545, fax: 383-0359, www.longboatkeyclub.com.* Golf aficionados rate it among the best in the US, with two challenging courses. Suites are luxurious, with private balconies overlooking the water or the fairways. Also pool, 38 tennis courts, fitness center, watersports. Wheelchair access. 232 rooms.

PANHANDLE

Seaside $$$–$$$$ *County Road 30-A, Seaside, FL 32459-473, tel: (850) 231-1320 or (800) 277-8696, fax: 231-2293, www.seasidefl.com.* Enclave of privately owned, fully furnished pastel accommodations available for rent. Whether you're staying in a spacious town home, a beachfront cottage or a penthouse, the beautiful beach is never far away. Pools, tennis courts, croquet, bikes to rent. Wheelchair access. 250 units.

Recommended Restaurants

Everywhere you turn, there's somewhere to eat, and almost all restaurants are open seven days a week. Here we give a selection of full-service restaurants, buffet restaurants, and food courts (multiple outlets sharing a table area). There is no space to list even a fraction of the vast number of restaurants and all-you-can-eat buffets well within our lowest price range (see also Eating Out, pages 96–100).

Each entry is marked with a symbol indicating the price range, per person, for a dinner comprising starter or salad, main course, and dessert. (Drinks, gratuities, and 6 percent sales tax are not included.)

$$$	$30 and over
$$	$15–30
$	up to $15

MIAMI AND MIAMI AREA

Azul $$–$$$ *Mandarin Oriental Hotel, 500 Brickell Key Dr., Brickell Key, tel: (305) 913-8288, www.mandarinoriental.com/miami.* The Mediterranean and Asia collide in a menu that offers an array of interesting dishes from Moroccan lamb to seared scallops and oysters wrapped in beef. Excellent service, great value, and fantastic views over Biscayne Bay.

Big Pink Café $ *157 Collins Ave., Miami Beach, tel: (305) 531-0888, www.bigpinkrestaurant.com.* Open daily, sometimes as late as 5am. Everything comes in large portions: salads, burgers, pastas, wood-burning oven pizzas, and banana cream pie – all made from scratch. Try the signature TV dinner on a stainless-steel tray with six compartments.

Havana Harry's $–$$ *4612 Le Juene Road, Coral Gables, tel: (305) 661-2622.* This place has one of the most extensive menus of tasty homestyle Cuban food, from mojito shredded pork sandwiches to guava barbecued chicken to palomilla steak smothered in onions. Big portions at reasonable prices.

Joe's Stone Crab $$$ *11 Washington Ave., Miami Beach, tel: (305) 673-0365, www.joesstonecrab.com.* Open only from October through May, daily for dinner, lunch Tuesday through Saturday. Joe's has been an institution since 1913, and serves fresh stone crab when it's in season. The wait for a table can seem interminable, so be patient. Take-out is also available and is a much quicker option.

News Café $$ *800 Ocean Dr., tel: (305) 538-6397, www.news cafe.com.* Must be the place to have breakfast or an afternoon break on South Beach. Its seaside terrace is full of visitors sipping a coffee or iced tea and reading the paper, or watching the waves and people come and go.

Versailles $–$$ *3555 SW 8th St., tel: (305) 444-0240, www. versaillescuban.com.* Black beans and rice, *ropa vieja* (shredded beef) and *café cubano* are among the staples at this no-frills eatery that is a magnet for some of Miami's most influential Cubans. It's open daily until 1am or later.

THE FLORIDA KEYS

Atlantic's Edge Dining Room $$$ *Cheeca Lodge, Mile Marker 82, Islamorada, tel: (305) 664-4651, www.cheeca.com/dining-atlantic-asp.* Lunch and dinner daily. Lovely dining room with views of the ocean, where the chef creates memorable seafood specialties like seafood ceviche with papaya, and roasted corn and crab soup.

Mangia, Mangia $ *900 Southard St., Key West, tel: (305) 294-2469, www.mangia-mangia.com.* Dinner daily. Locals frequent this family-run Italian/American eatery, a Chicago-style pasta place with superb home-made noodles.

Mrs Mac's Kitchen $$ *Mile Marker 99, Key Largo, tel: (305) 451-3722, www.mrsmacskitchen.com.* A traditional roadside café with license plate decor serving all-day breakfasts and large portions of nostalgia. Open for breakfast, lunch and dinner.

SOUTHEAST FLORIDA/THE GOLD COAST

Cap's Place $–$$ *2765 NE 28th Court, Lighthouse Point (Ft. Lauderdale, Pompano area), tel: (954) 941-0418, www.caps place.com.* Dinner daily. This historic landmark dates back to the 1920s, when the building was a speakeasy. Cap's is on a small intracoastal island, but many celebrities have found their way here since the place opened in 1928. Try the hearts of palm (harvested from the center of the palm tree), a tasty and rare treat. Fresh fish is recommended.

TooJay's Gourmet Deli $ *313 Royal Poinciana Plaza, Poinciana Center, Palm Beach, tel: (561) 659-7232, www.toojays.com.* Open daily. Overstuffed sandwiches and delicatessen favorites in a relaxed atmosphere. At dinner, the menu expands with giant portions of chicken pot pie, stuffed cabbage and other home-style dishes.

CENTRAL EAST AND NORTHEAST FLORIDA

95 Cordova $$$–$$$$ *Casa Monica Hotel, 95 Cordova St., St Augustine, tel: (904) 810-6810, www.casamonica.com/95cordova.* Hotel eateries often don't fill the plate, but this is one that delivers an international meat and seafood menu with a respectable wine list.

Aunt Catfish's $–$$ *4009 Halifax Drive, Port Orange, tel: (386) 767-4768, www.auntcatfishontheriver.com.* Lunch and dinner. Nearly any seafood imaginable – shrimp, lobster, crabs, scallops, oysters, and fish – is on the bountiful menu. Then they'll ask if you want it prepared Cajun-style, fried, broiled, grilled, or baked. The choices are nearly endless.

Dixie Crossroads $–$$ *1475 Garden St., Titusville, tel: (321) 268-5000, www.nbbd.com/dixiecrossroads.* Lunch and dinner daily. There's always a line at this popular seafood palace, but just relax and nibble on one of their famous corn fritters that they pass around to those waiting for tables. Dixie Crossroads is known for generous servings and the white shrimp caught in local waters.

Florida House Inn and Restaurant $ *20 and 22 S. Third St., Fernandina Beach (Amelia Island), tel: (904) 261-3300, www.florida houseinn.com.* For a true Southern dinner, join the crowd at the Florida House, where they pass around steaming bowls of collard greens, black-eyed peas, fried chicken, and more. The long wooden tables encourage great conversation.

WALT DISNEY WORLD

Artist Point $$ *Disney's Wilderness Lodge Resort, Walt Disney World, tel: (407) WDW-DINE, www.disneyworld.com.* It's easy to imagine you've been transported to the Pacific Northwest in this restaurant. The menu takes advantage of the diverse harvest from the coastlines of Washington, Oregon, and British Columbia. Specialties include sautéed elk sausage, cedar-roasted wild king salmon, venison chops and pan-seared rainbow trout.

California Grill $$ *Disney's Contemporary Resort, Walt Disney World, tel: (407) WDW-DINE, www.disneyworld.com.* Dinner nightly. Art Nouveau-inspired dining room on the 15th floor is Disney's most popular, but it's worth the wait for the simple, sophisticated cooking. Starting with the pristine sushi or a crisp, thin-crust pizza.

Cítricos $$$ *Disney's Grand Floridian Resort & Spa, Walt Disney World, tel: (407) WDW-DINE, www.disneyworld.com.* Dinner nightly. Inviting Mediterranean ambience blends seamlessly with the food of Chef Roland Muller. Try the tender braised veal shank with orzo and soy glaze.

Coral Reef Restaurant $$ *The Living Seas pavilion, Epcot, Walt Disney World, tel: (407) WDW-DINE, www.disneyworld.com.* Dine in one of the most unusual restaurants in the world, with a 5.7-million-gallon saltwater aquarium as the backdrop. Diners look out into the waters through eight-story-high windows to see nearly 3,000 specimens of Caribbean reef life, with the occasional diver swimming past. The menu continues the ocean theme with fresh seafood flown in from around the world.

House of Blues $$–$$$ *1490 E. Buena Vista Dr., Lake Buena Vista, tel: (407) 934-2583, www.hob.com.* The daily menus are nothing to ignore, but the legendary Sunday gospel brunch is a foot-stomping smash.

Jiko $$–$$$ *Disney's Animal Kingdom Lodge, Walt Disney World, tel: (407) WDW-DINE, www.disneyworld.com.* The African fusion menu includes lamb in phyllo, shrimp curry with tomatoes and artichokes, and an extensive South African wine list make this a very popular refueling stop for Disney guests.

Spoodles $$ *Disney's BoardWalk Inn & Villas, Walt Disney World, tel: (407) WDW-DINE, www.disneyworld.com.* Open daily. An open kitchen and big wooden tables bring to mind a casual Mediterranean eatery. We recommend grazing instead of ordering full entrées: Try the Moroccan spiced tuna with fennel, lemon, chives, and spiced olive oil.

Victoria & Albert's $$$ *Disney's Grand Floridian Resort & Spa, Walt Disney World, tel: (407) WDW-DINE, www.disneyworld. com.* Dinner nightly. This is the only Disney restaurant that requires men to wear a jacket, but don't be put off by the formality. The dining room seats just 60, and the chef takes his time with every guest. The menu changes daily based on what's freshest at the market.

ORLANDO AREA

Dux $$$ *Peabody Hotel, 9801 International Drive, Orlando, tel: (407) 345-4550.* The finest dining experience on International Drive is found in this restaurant named after the Peabody's resident fowl.

Emeril's Restaurant Orlando $$$ *6000 Universal Blvd., CityWalk at Universal Studios Escape, tel: (407) 224-2424, www.emerils.com.* One of America's most flamboyant chefs, Emeril Lagasse, opened this outpost of his New Orleans restaurant at Universal Studios Escape. If you're in the mood for high-calorie cooking, get in line. Try the Louisiana Oyster Stew.

Hot Olives $$–$$$ *463 W. New England Ave., Winter Park, tel: (407) 629-1030, www.hotolivesrestaurant.com/index.html.* Experimental cuisine rules in this trendy bistro, where spicy black olives are breaded, stuffed with asiago cheese and served with blue cheese, and chicken arrives with lemon capers. It's a great place to get out of the routine.

Seasons 52 $$–$$$ *7700 West Sand Lake Road, Orlando, tel: (407) 354-5212, www.seasons52.com.* This relatively new arrival near Universal Orlando delivers flavor and a health-conscious, seasonally changing menu.

SOUTHWEST FLORIDA

The Bubble Room $$ *15001 Captiva Drive, Captiva Island, tel: (239) 472-5558, www.bubbleroomrestaurant.com.* Lunch and dinner daily. The Bubble Room has been a popular family choice for years, packed with movie stills, and all sorts of kitsch, including puppets, toy trains, and old jukeboxes. Though the food is not exactly haute cuisine, there's plenty of it, so consider sharing a plate.

Rod & Gun Club $ *200 Riverside Drive, Everglades City, tel: (239) 695-2101, www.evergladesrodandgun.com.* Open daily. This 130-year-old lodge caters mostly to fishermen, but the restaurant is a great stop after a day in the Everglades, with fresh seafood – try the southern-fried grouper – lobster salad, stone crabs, and frog legs. The tart Key lime pie is worth the calories. No credit cards.

Shula's Steak House $$$ *5111 Tamiami Trail North, Naples. tel: (239) 430-4999, www.donshula.com.* Located at the Naples Hilton Hotel & Towers, this is one of a chain of steakhouses throughout Florida. Each serves up prime Angus beef, available in huge portions, if requested, along with Maine lobster and even a few selections for non-beef-eaters. Named for the former coach of the Miami Dolphins professional football team, the restaurant is sometimes visited by Coach Shula himself.

CENTRAL WEST FLORIDA

Bern's Steak House $$$ *1208 S. Howard Ave., Tampa, tel: (813) 251-2421, www.bernssteakhouse.com.* Reservations are a must at this mecca for meat-lovers. First you must decide the weight and thickness of your steak, then peruse the 200,000-bottle wine collection. Most vegetables are grown in the restaurant's own organic garden.

Columbia Restaurant $–$$ *2117 E. 7th Ave., Ybor City, tel: (813) 248-4961, www.columbiarestaurant.com.* In the same location since 1905, the Columbia is known as 'America's Oldest Spanish Restaurant.' It's a huge place, spanning an entire city block in the heart of Ybor City. Despite its size, the food is excellent, particularly the black bean soup, boliche, and the '1905' salad. There is also a nightly flamenco performance here to entertain guests.

Crab & Fin $$ *420 St Armand's Circle, Sarasota, tel: (941) 388-3964, www.crabfinrestaurant.com.* Open daily. Crab claws, crab cakes, crab salad – this is the place for crustacean lovers, as well as a huge range of other seafood. Also home-made pasta, meat, and vegetarian alternatives on the menu. A pianist keeps the crowd lively. There's also a dessert room upstairs.

PANHANDLE

Boss Oyster $ *125 Water St., Apalachicola, tel: (850) 653-9364, www.apalachicolariverinn.com/boss.html.* Lunch and dinner daily. Apalachicola is famous for its oysters, and this is the place to sit out on the waterfront and try them. All of the seafood is incredibly fresh, and fried seafood platters are popular. This is a true Florida experience.

Criolla's $$–$$$ *170 E. C30-A, Santa Rosa Beach, near Seaside, tel: (850) 267-1267, www.criollas.com.* Open nightly for dinner. This award-winning restaurant is pricey, but well worth it. You won't be disappointed with any fish, and save room for the from-scratch desserts.

INDEX

Berlitz pocket guide

Florida

Seventh Edition 2009
Reprinted 2011

Written by Martin Gostelow
Updated by Christina Tourigny and Jim Tunstall
Series Editor: Tom Stainer

Photography credits
Alamy 17, 47; Tony Arruza 33; Bancroft Library 15; © Disney Enterprises, Inc. 54, 57; Mary Evans Picture Library 14; Florida Division of Tourism 21; Glyn Genin 97; Martin Gostelow 25; istock 81; Library of Congress 19; Miami and Greater Fort Lauderdale Convention and Visitors Bureau 89; Richard Nowitz 6, 9, 10, 11, 22, 51, 53, 58, 60, 61, 63, 64, 71, 74, 75, 78, 79, 85, 86, 91, 92, 99, 100; Orlando Orange County 44; Palm Beach Tourism 42, 43; Mark Read 72, 80; Seaworld Orlando 68; State Library and Archives of Florida 12; Universal Orlando 66, 94; Gregory Wrona 24, 26, 29, 31, 32, 34, 35, 37, 39, 40, 49, 69, 77, 82
Cover picture: 4Corners Images

Contact us

At Berlitz we strive to keep our guides as accurate and up to date as possible, but if you find anything that has changed, or if you have any suggestions on ways to improve this guide, then we would be delighted to hear from you.

Berlitz Publishing, PO Box 7910, London SE1 1WE, England.
email: berlitz@apaguide.co.uk
www.berlitzpublishing.com